Torrential Love

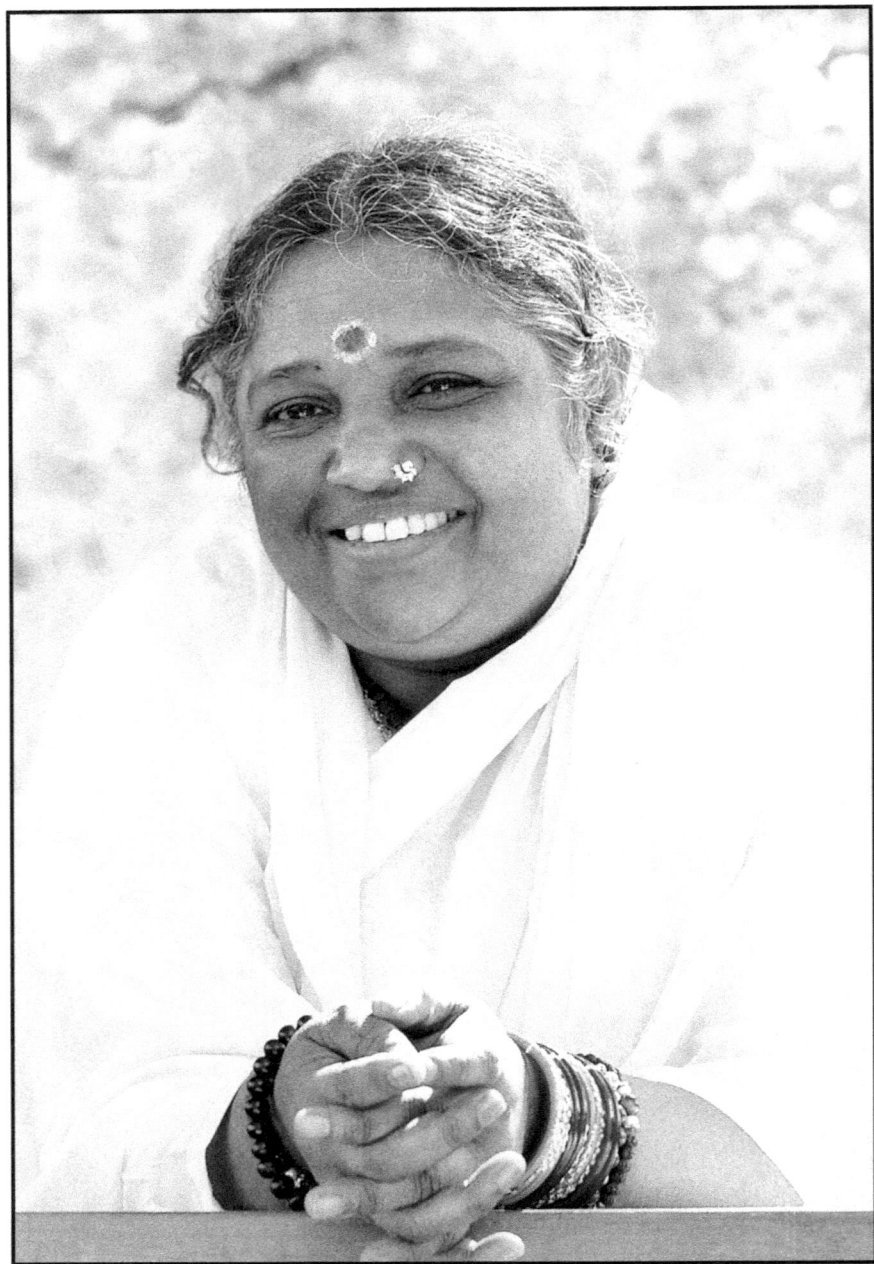

Torrential Love

Swamini Krishnamrita Prana

Mata Amritanandamayi Center, San Ramon
California, United States

Torrential Love

By Swamini Krishnamrita Prana

Published by:
Mata Amritanandamayi Center
P.O. Box 613
San Ramon, CA 94583
United States

In India:
www.amritapuri.org
inform@amritapuri.org

In Europe:
www.amma-europe.org

In US:
www.amma.org

If all the land
Were turned to paper,
And all the seas
Turned to ink,
And all the forests
Into pens to write with,
They would still not suffice
To describe
The greatness of the Guru.

Kabir

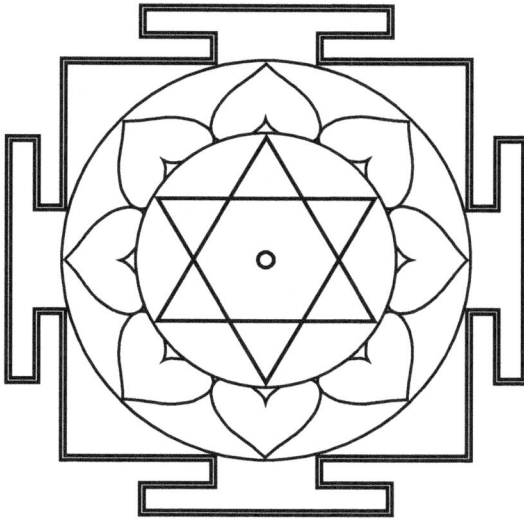

Contents

Introduction

*Without love and compassion the world cannot
exist. The whole of existence is indebted to
the Mahatmas for the love and compassion
they have showered on all of creation.*

Amma

Some Saints are born only to bless this earth with their holy
presence. They may spend their years sitting quietly in isolated Himalayan caves, absorbed in peaceful meditation, and
receiving only those who happen to come across them.

But another kind of *Mahatma* comes to this world spe-
cifically to actively alleviate suffering by uplifting the human
race. Merged with Divine Consciousness, this Self-realized
Soul could choose to stay absorbed in that Supreme level of
God-intoxication and simply forget about the rest of us. But
instead, he or she desires to descend to our level to personally
transform our afflictions into remembrance of our true nature.

Like a precious diamond, this Mahatma resides not deep
in a cave, nor in the tranquil forests or beautiful mountains.
This benevolent Soul comes to us like the holy Ganges river,
flowing throughout the land, even to dark corners of dirty cities, hastening to come in touch with the forgotten and down-
trodden. Ever-pure and unchanging, like the river, a Mahatma
such as Amma blesses all of humanity with Her purifying
touch wherever She goes. The river does not care what people

do with her water – some may worship it, others may spit in it. Still, her hallowed nature remains unchanged, for it simply overflows from the Source.

Amma is a rare jewel who has come down to try and gently set us free. Her nature overflows with compassion that She extends to all She comes into contact with. She has affectionately consoled and comforted more than 28 million people and Her embraces continue to flow out to the poor and the wealthy, the sick and the well. She cannot help Herself.

Just like the water from a cool mountain spring may quench the thirst of one dying in the desert, so the love of a fully God-realized Soul comes as sweet nectar to ease the pain of this mortal existence.

When people come to Amma, they may ask for many things – blessings for their health, their family, their work. Amma helps them with these individual needs while emphasizing, "There is one thing in this world that if you have, then all the rest will come along with it – this one thing is Love." Amma teaches:

> Love is within everyone, even inside the cruelest person, but most are not able to share this love, lying trapped inside of us. A large majority of people in this world did not receive enough love as a child. Even while they were in the womb they might not have received love from their mother and this lack of love has deeply affected them. Every person has a right to the unlimited wealth of love and kindness. No matter how much we draw from this spring, it will never go dry – the more kindness and love we give, the more it will increase.

Because we have not experienced this pure love, we often find life to be incredibly difficult. Sometimes we may feel like we are trapped within a burning building – burning from within us, as well as without. It is in this very moment of despair that the holy presence of Amma comes as a cooling breeze to extinguish the fire.

There is a young child who lives at *Amritapuri*. He sometimes follows Amma closely, along with many others. Although he is not quite three years old, he will try to keep up with Her, toddling alongside Her, as he veers off to one side and then the other. Amma patiently helps him along by pulling him back on the path, straightening him out, walking behind him if She has to, redirecting him. She does the same for us, patiently guiding us in the right direction when we wander off our path, gently steering us toward our goal.

We are all walking on the same journey through life but sometimes we forget where we are trying to go. Amma comes again and again to guide us back to our final destination.

People often ask me what it is like to live with Amma and travel around the world with Her. To be honest, it is not something that one can easily express in words. Through such a limited medium as language, it is extremely difficult to try to convey the profound feelings and impressions that rise up from within when the heart is so deeply touched and opened.

All I can do is try to share a few of the beautiful gems that have been offered in front of me by Amma. Every word that emanates from Her is like a priceless treasure. When such treasures are offered in front of us, how can we help but hold out our hands to try to hold them, to share with others the beauty we have received from Amma.

I have spent more than half of this lifetime living with Amma – yet She remains entirely beyond my comprehension. Just when I might think that I am starting to understand Her, She will prove me totally wrong. When I might think that I have unmasked another layer from the veils that hide Her, I find several more may appear to replace it.

After finishing my first book, *Sacred Journey*, I was delighted to see how much it helped people feel connected to Amma. I felt that if in this life I had done at least that one good thing to glorify the name of Amma, then the book was worthwhile. My hope is that readers will equally enjoy this second offering, and ultimately experience the torrential love that flows from the ambrosial jewel that is Amma.

Chapter 1

The Beginning

Some call it Amma, some call it by other names.
But this remains the same, unchanged, unaffected.
No one can pierce the mystery of this Being.

Amma

When Amma was born, the way of life in Her small fishing community had remained unchanged for decades. Few visitors and certainly no foreigners ever entered the village in those days. Amma's mother Damayanti was deeply devout and performed traditional spiritual practices daily. The Lord's name was always on her lips. She arose at three every morning, woke her children and then picked fresh flowers to make garlands to offer to God during her worship. Every week she undertook fasts on specific days for different deities.

Before Amma's birth, Damayanti told her husband that she had a recurring dream that Lord Krishna entered her in the form of a divine light, and that this light surrounded everything around her. When she told this to *Sugunachan*, he replied that this was nothing special. "Because you chant *mantras* 20 hours a day and think of God all the time, what is strange about that?" But Damayanti Amma said that she had never had dreams like this before, and she had already given birth to several other children.

"I am sure the child in me is very special," she said to her husband. However, Achan refused to believe her. Instead, he made fun of her, and soon went to sleep.

Amazingly, that night he had a similar dream. Amma's father only occasionally visited temples or chanted mantras, so when he had the same dream-experience, he too became convinced that the child his wife was carrying was someone divine. Every day he touched Damayanti's stomach and did *pranams* to the child within her. He later said that her stomach was the purest place in the world since Amma was born from it.

From the time that Amma was very young, She proved to be surprisingly different from other children. As an infant of just a few months, Amma gazed intensely at all the photos of saints and different Gods and Goddesses that adorned the walls of Her family home. Her father said that She would stare at the photos for a long time and then cry, although not like any of their other children cried.

As a little girl, Amma built temples in the sand and gathered all the other children around Her to play and worship at these temples. In the village where Amma grew up, no one was educated in the *Sanskrit* language. But somehow Amma possessed this profound knowledge, and She taught Sanskrit mantras to the other children. No one knew or practiced meditation, and yet at a very early age Amma sat in meditation. Her family thought that She was asleep, but still they wondered how She could sleep sitting in an upright position.

When Amma was about seven years old, She sometimes cried intensely without stopping, lost in Her own world of devotion and longing for God. She wanted to go to an isolated place so that She could cry to God without people disturbing Her. Her father saw Her like this and tried to console Her. He picked Her up and held Her against his shoulder to try and comfort Her. She asked Her father to take Her to the Himalayas. He assured that he would do so, and told Her to try to get some rest. She fell asleep against his shoulder innocently believing that he would take Her there. Later when She awoke She found that She was not in the Himalayas and started crying all over again.

Amma attended a primary school that was a ten-minute walk from Her house. Every morning She started out for school at least one hour early, but She always arrived after the others, and often late. One day the teachers became annoyed at Her tardiness and decided to tell Her father about it. Sugunachan could not account for his daughter's behavior, and so he secretly investigated. He discovered that Amma was visiting all the houses of the poor along the way to school, to see how they were and to help them if needed. She gave away whatever She could acquire from Her own house to these disadvantaged people. If anyone questioned Her about what She was giving away, She admitted nothing at the beginning and only in the very end revealed what She had done.

At that time there was an old man who wandered around to all of the houses in the village. He played his small drum and begged for money. Amma always called him "father," which really irritated Her family. One day, Amma's father hung his new *dhoti* on the clothesline. Later when he came back to collect it, he found an old dhoti in its place. Several times, both Amma's father and Her elder brother found their new clothes gone and some old ones in their place. They had no idea what was going on, until one day Amma was caught red-handed taking Her father's new dhoti and replacing it with the beggar's old one. She got a good beating that day.

When Amma was in the fourth grade, She often had terrible stomach aches. One time it was so bad that She had to leave school to go home to recover. Due to the unbearable pain Amma ended up rolling on the floor. Her father became worried and crossed over the backwaters to bring back a doctor from the village.

When he arrived, the doctor had medicines and an injection with him. When Amma saw the large syringe She refused to take the injection. Her rebellious behavior made Her father angry because he had gone to a lot of trouble to go and fetch the doctor. Concerned that the doctor might be annoyed for being troubled unnecessarily, he said that She must at least take some of the medicine. Amma reluctantly agreed and accepted a large tablet with a glass of water. After this, Amma insisted that She was fine and the stomach pain had disappeared. A few hours later She went outside to play. It was then that Her father discovered the wet tablet that Amma had spit out and hidden under Her bed. He shook his head. *She is an incorrigible child,* he thought to himself.

In those days, Amma's father was often away from home on fishing trips. Whenever he returned, his wife had a long list of complaints about the latest trouble Amma had given her. On one such occasion when Amma was lying down asleep, Her mother quietly complained to him about all the mischievous things that She had done. Amma suddenly spoke out strongly, saying, "I am not your daughter-in-law!"[1] Her father recalls that Amma then repeated very seriously, "I know everything!"

---

[1] Traditionally daughters-in-law are not treated with the same respect as biological daughters.

Her father thought that Amma meant She knew everything in Her school textbook, so he brought the book over to Her. The brand new book, hardly touched, still smelled fresh from the printing press. He asked Amma to prove what She had just said and to repeat what was in the book. Amma started to repeat all of the contents in the book, to Her father's absolute amazement, for he knew that She had probably never even looked in it. Amma's elder sister studied in a higher grade so Her father brought over her more advanced book and started to test Amma. Once again, to his surprise, She repeated everything in Her sister's book as well.

Shocked by Her brilliance, Amma's parents felt that they must make sure to educate Her very well. But this was not to happen, as Amma's mother fell ill and She had to leave school in the fourth grade to supervise the household.

Even though Amma no longer attended school, She still learned some of the lessons taught there because She helped Her brothers and sisters with their school work. Her responsibilities included taking care of Her siblings, getting them up and ready for school, feeding them, and doing all the household work as well. She was like the family servant.

Amma went out daily to buy the provisions for the family. She was given a small amount of money and was expected to cover all household expenses with it for one week. In this way, Amma first learned the value of everything and how to organize household expenses on an extremely small budget. What She learned as a young girl helped form the foundation of Her knowledge and management skills for running an *ashram* and various service organizations.

The village where Amma grew up was situated on a narrow strip of land between the Arabian Sea and the backwaters. The

village covered about ten acres of land, with about 100 huts built very close together. Children often played at each other's houses, and their mothers did not worry about them as they knew they were safe somewhere nearby.

For at least six months of the year, the usually brackish backwaters were full of fresh water so the children had fun jumping and swimming in the water. They also climbed trees to pick mangoes. When they heard the wind blowing, they rushed to the trees and sat under them praying intensely for the tiny mangoes to fall.

Amma fondly remembers these times from Her childhood. Just recently, while we were driving away from the end of a *darshan* program, some children ran after the car trying to keep up with it, crying out in excitement. Amma said that it reminded Her of Her younger days when all the children ran and played together and tried to find mangoes. She said that while She is giving darshan, sometimes She hears the cries of young children playing outside and it reminds Her again of Her younger days.

Amma was often sent to a neighboring house to get fire for cooking or to light the oil lamp. In those days, the villagers did not use matches. Instead, they took fire from whichever house already had their kitchen stove burning. Amma's mother instructed Her that when She went into a house and saw dirty dishes, before taking the fire She should first wash the dishes or clean up the house. In those earlier days, the villagers had this kind of consideration for each other. They did not really know anything about spirituality, but the attitude of looking out for each other was always inherent in their upbringing.

When She was growing up Amma had no formal teacher to turn to, so for Her, everything became a spiritual lesson. She learned from all of life's experiences.

As a young girl, when the breeze touched Her skin, She used to feel that it was God embracing Her. Amma said that She would always talk to Mother Nature, to Her pillow, to everything. There was nothing for Her that was not filled with the Divine Consciousness.

She loved to be by the seashore and looked upon the ocean as Her mother. She used to sit near the water and tell her everything, as the ocean was the only one that could understand Her. Sometimes She would take some bread and something to drink, and after meditation She would offer it to the sea, wanting to share everything with her.

As a child, Amma went from house to house every day to gather food scraps for feeding Her family's cows. At many of the houses She saw tremendous suffering. If the fishermen did not catch any fish for a few days, then often their families starved. Families were large in those days, perhaps having 12 children. Sometimes Amma saw distraught mothers holding onto their children, all of them crying. The children cried from hunger, and the mother cried because she had nothing to give them; while in other houses people had more than enough to eat. This disparity often confused Amma and made Her cry out in anger at a God that could show such partiality. But the answer came back to Her that these people suffered because of their *karma*, and although it was their karma to suffer, it was also Her *dharma* to show compassion.

Amma never questioned if God really existed or not. To Her the question was, *How can I relieve the suffering that goes on everywhere?* After seeing such adversity, Amma knew from a very early age that Her life was meant to be given as a gift to uplift humanity.

Amma has said that She never saw a *sannyasin* in the local area at all until She was around 20 years old. The only temple for the people was situated seven kilometers away in a place called Oachira. Once every year Her father used to take his eight children for the annual festival that was held there. It was like heaven for them to go on this yearly pilgrimage.

Until She was 19 years old, She had traveled no further than the 13 kilometers to Her grandmother's house. At 22, She made the 35 kilometer journey to Kollam, but no further. Although She never traveled far in Her youth, Amma now spends most of Her time traveling the length and breadth of the world each year, bringing comfort and joy wherever She goes.

Chapter 2

Beyond Religion

*We have learned to fly the air like birds and swim
the sea like fish – but we have not learned the simple
art of living together like brothers and sisters.*
Martin Luther King Jr.

People often wonder how Amma first began to give Her darshan. Amma says that it was never planned, but just spontaneously started to happen when the poor villagers came crying to Her because of their problems. Amma deeply identified Herself with them. She totally shared their sorrows and tried to console and comfort them so that they could find some relief. She started by putting them on Her lap, caressing them and then embracing them as a mother would comfort her own child.

Other villagers who also had problems saw Amma giving so much affection and complained, "She hugged that person so She should hug me!" And they demanded comfort as well. As a result Amma started to console one person after another and in this way the tradition of the darshan line began. Amma became like a river of love ceaselessly flowing, embracing all who came to Her filled with sorrow.

In Amma's village, people lived in thatched huts made from coconut leaves. Since the leaves would wear thin, causing the roofs to leak, they would need to be re-thatched every year before the monsoon season. But some villagers could not afford the 1,000 rupees that it cost to re-thatch their roofs every year. When it rained at night, if they did not have enough vessels to catch the falling water, they would have to sit inside their huts holding umbrellas over their sleeping children.

When Amma was growing up She often had to take Her younger brother to the local hospital because of his poor health. At the hospital She saw people suffering because they could not afford to spend any money on pain medication. The facilities in the hospital were meager and sometimes due to lack of electricity things were not sterilized properly and instruments such as needles were used over and over again.

The hospital required that the patients have a small piece of paper for the doctor to write their name, details and a prescription to give to the pharmacist. But some people were so poor that they could not even afford the paper to give to the doctor to write on and as a result were unable to collect the medicine.

Amma also saw poor families that did not have money to buy their children sheets of paper to submit the answers to their school examinations. These children had to go without an education due to the lack of a few rupees.

Because of this, Amma used to tear pages out of Her sisters' school books to give to these poor people so they could receive their medication or take their exams. When Her sisters found out what She had done, they often beat Her, but still this did not stop Her from trying to help the poor.

Amma saw a great amount of suffering during Her childhood. As a result of witnessing so much hardship throughout

Her early life, the first thing that Amma said when the Amritapuri ashram was registered as a charitable institution in 1983 was, "Do not make me like a caged parrot. Do not make this organization like a business firm. It should stand for the people, for the suffering humanity." Right from the very beginning, through all the years and until this very day, that ideal has been absolutely and uncompromisingly upheld by Amma and all the people that work in service for Her.

People are so inspired by Amma. Even the poorest of the poor may try to press a one-rupee coin in Her hand when they come for darshan in India, knowing that She will use it to serve others. They cannot really offer much more than this, but they also want to help others and know that Amma will do it on their behalf. She says they are like small birds making offerings, and everything altogether becomes a river-like flow.

The great Masters will take examples from worldly life and break them down so that people can understand them. The Supreme Truth, although extremely simple in essence, remains beyond our grasp, intangible because of its simplicity. It is like a huge piece of rock candy that is broken down and given to us in bite-size pieces. Others claim to understand the nature of rock candy and have plenty to say about the rock candy. They may have even licked the outside of it, but have never experienced its full sweetness. They cannot break down the principles to its true essentials for us to digest. Only an enlightened teacher like Amma can manage to do this for us.

In the Hindu tradition, people break coconuts in front of the temple to symbolize the breaking of the ego. This action signifies, "Oh God, I am trying to break the ego in front of You!" And just as sweet water comes out of the broken coconut, so joy emerges when the ego is surrendered.

Amma has said that all symbols of Hinduism have deep and significant meanings. The external symbolism within Hinduism helps one to gain concentration of the mind and develop discipline. For example, the *vibhuti* that is applied to the forehead is medicinal, and symbolizes that everything is eventually reduced to ashes and therefore impermanent. The pores on the forehead have special nerve endings and will absorb the ashes. Likewise, lighting the camphor and waving it during the *arati* signifies the relinquishing of one's ego. Just as camphor burns without leaving a residue, when we offer our selves, when we offer our egos wholeheartedly, in that surrender our individuality burns away.

People have often asked what the connection is between Amma and Hinduism. Amma says that because She was brought up in Hindu culture and has fully understood its inner significance, She feels that it is beneficial for anybody who is interested. Amma never forces anyone to worship Gods or Goddesses. She advises us to see God in everybody, to worship each and every aspect of creation. She repeats again and again that creation and the Creator are not two, but are one and the same.

When Amma gives *satsangs* at public programs in India, She often tries to teach people the real meaning behind the Gods and Goddesses and different concepts of *Sanatana Dharma*. Most people have blindly accepted rituals without understanding the true meaning behind them. Amma reminds people to try to follow the real meaning of their own religion. One need not change their religion, but should instead strive to understand its underlying essence.

One day while traveling through London we had to catch a taxi to another terminal. Noticing our Indian dress, the taxi driver who was of African descent asked me what religion we were. I laughed, as this is always a difficult question to answer. For someone like Amma who has totally gone beyond the confines of any religion and is trying to teach us to do the same, it is misleading to say that we are simply Hindus, but it is difficult to explain this effectively to others and expect them to understand.

Trying to avoid being categorized into the label of one particular religion, I replied that our religion was love and service to humanity. I could see by his expression that he was not really satisfied with my answer. I knew he wanted to hear a label that he was familiar with, and so I acquiesced and finally replied, "Hindu."

Satisfied with this answer he then asked what we thought about what happens when we die, and where do we go? Amma's answer to him was in the form of a question. "What happens when it rains? Where does that water go to?"

The taxi driver thought about it for a while and then answered, "Well it just goes around – and then comes back." Ah! Yes! He got it, he answered his own question and we all laughed.

By this point we had reached our destination and had gotten out of the taxi and were just starting to enter the building. His spiritual curiosity aroused, the driver darted a final question. He asked, "Where is God?" Amma replied that man had cut him up and called it religion.

If we look at the newspapers on any day, in any part of the world we will see incredible acts of violence and destruction. People want to kill and maim others in the name of their religion. Amma points out that a good number are ready to die for their religion, but how many are ready to live for their

religion, in the true essence of the purity contained within it? Hardly anybody, so it seems.

We tend to see only the outside of religion. We do not see the inside of religion, the essence of religion, which *is* spirituality. But once we can imbibe and practice that essence, then things will be different. Lack of spiritual experience has created all the divisions that we see in society.

Amma says that in the attitude of "I am a Hindu," "I am a Christian," "I am a Muslim," the small "I", the ego, is still there. We must strive to transcend this attitude. This inquiry into the real "I" will take us to the Truth. It is for knowing this "I," for knowing the Self, that we do our various spiritual practices.

Amma points out that there is no use in mere studying and thinking of *Vedanta*. We have to live Vedanta and show that it is practical. For example, we should feel others as ourselves and try to help them and thus uplift them so that all in this world will be happy. This is the fundamental spiritual principle behind the mantra *Lokah Samastah Sukhino Bhavantu* – May all beings in all the worlds be happy.

Religion and spirituality are the means to open our hearts and express love and compassion to others. But because of our wrong understanding and selfishness we end up misusing them and creating even more problems. The main purpose of life is to live happily and to experience true peace of mind while being focused on the present moment. But with all the freedom that people think they have – how much peace of mind is really there? Most people are suffering terribly.

Amma frequently has to remind us that the only way we will find true lasting freedom is from within. Once we find that freedom, it will never leave us. But we can find it only through spirituality.

Amma says that love cannot be explained in words because it is simply beyond the power of words – it is pure experience. Just as we cannot explain the sound of thunder and rain, but we have to experience it. When we start giving love, love awakens inside of us and there is no longer "two," they become united as only "one."

Unfortunately, most people remain divided. In today's world there is an incredible amount of turmoil and conflict. People often want to blame religion as the cause. But Amma says that such accusations are not correct. It is the misinterpretations of religion that create the problems, not spirituality, which is the fundamental nature of all religions.

After a press interview one day, the reporter was so impressed by Amma. He remarked that Her answers were utterly simple but extremely profound. Amma's reply was that She had grown up in a village and had not studied anything – but She had come to know Herself. In that knowing of Herself, She came to truly understand everyone else, since we are not isolated entities but are all connected like the links in a chain.

If one drops a stone in a pond, then all the ripples will travel out to the edges of the pond. Once they reach the edge they will return to the middle again. So it is if we study; we learn so much but eventually we have to come back to the point from where we started to realize that we do not really know anything.

Amma gives the example that it only takes a small key to open a lock. If we try to stick other things in it to open it, then the lock will only get broken. In this way the Supreme Truth is actually very simple – but we always try to complicate it.

There are many different religions but God is only one. There is no caste or creed for Pure Consciousness. The paths to reach the truth are countless but the goal is one and the same. Similarly, people perform various practices to reach the same truth.

Amma never tries to influence anybody to accept what they feel uncomfortable practicing. She compassionately advises each one according to their own mental constitution and their own culture. For those who worship Christ, Amma initiates them in the mantra of Jesus Christ. For those who practice Islam, Amma gives them the mantra of Allah. And for those who worship the formless, Amma initiates them with an appropriate mantra.

When a catastrophic earthquake hit Kashmir in October 2005, some of Amma's representatives were sent to the border area to try to see what could be done to help. Before they left, Amma instructed them that they were not to talk about Amma, as most devotees are inclined to do, but instead they should simply try to comfort the people with spiritual guidance according to the religion of those people. After distributing food and clothing to those who were in need, the volunteers sat with the local people who had lost their homes and they all sang together. The songs were carefully chosen so as not to conflict with the Muslim faith. This really opened the people's hearts to a love that encompassed all humanity and was not confined to just one religion.

Amma said that in a calamity we should go to the level of the people suffering and try to become one with them, but that we should never try to change another's religion. We should help people to believe more firmly in their own faith and help them call out to God according to their own understanding and customs.

Chapter 3

A Perfect Master

*A mere touch or glance from a Mahatma can
benefit us far more than ten years of practicing
austerities. But to experience that benefit, we have
to get rid of the ego and we need to have faith.*

Amma

Amma's paternal grandmother was a very pious woman.
She spent most of her life making flower garlands for the
kalari. When she came to Amma for darshan, Amma lovingly
teased her by filling the big holes in her earlobes with flowers.
The years melted away as Amma's grandmother became like a
young girl in front of her divine grandchild.

Even at the age of ninety-plus, Amma's grandmother arose
early in the morning. She walked around the Amritapuri
ashram collecting flowers for the kalari. Her back badly bent
over from arthritis, she could only move very slowly. Still she
made her way without help around the ashram. Until just two
years before her death, she heated up the water for her daily
bath herself. It was only at the end of her life that she became
too weak to care for herself and was admitted to the ashram
hospital where she spent the last of her days.

Even while she was in an unconscious state in the hospital, her hands would take her sari and twist the cloth in the same way that she had used her hands to make garlands. Because she had done this in the morning hours for many years, this action was so deeply embedded in her mind that she still performed it even when she was unconscious. Let us hope that by the time we get old we will have picked up some good habits.

The future is always in our own hands. As Buddha once said, "What you are – is what you have been. But what you will be is what you do now. If you want to know your past lives, look into your present condition. If you want to know your future, then look into your present actions."

If we can develop good thoughts within us, little by little the bad thoughts will disappear. It is similar to what happens to a vessel of seawater when we add fresh water – the water becomes less salty.

When it snows in the mountains we feel that the beautiful snowflakes are quite harmless. But when these snowflakes melt, they start flowing down the mountains like a swollen river. That flow can carry huge boulders that could even wash us away. Similarly, we might feel that one thought is insignificant, that it has no power, but as that thought gets strengthened, it gets translated into action and can cause irreparable damage and disaster. We have to be aware of negative thoughts in the mind and try to stop them in the beginning stage, before they grow and can cause harm.

As long as we remain identified with the body and mind we need to lead some kind of disciplined life. The practice of discipline can help to create awareness in the mind. Still, it is very difficult to transcend *vasanas* (negative tendencies) on our own, which is why we need the help of a perfect Master.

Amma says we need not worry about past actions. Like an eraser can erase whatever a pencil writes, the Master can take away all our mistakes. But we must take care not to keep repeating the same mistakes. For if we keep writing and erasing in the same place over and over again the paper will eventually tear.

When we have come to a perfect Master and have gained true surrender, we have nothing more to worry about. Amma knows that it is difficult to have total surrender. She says that total surrender is, in fact, God-realization. Even though absolute surrender is difficult to attain, we ought to at least put forth our best effort. The capacity to do this depends on the spiritual evolution of each and every person at their respective levels. Everything in life is God's creation – except our ego. The ego is our own creation. To remove the ego we need the help of someone from outside of our own creation. We need a perfect Master. The *Guru* alone can remove the cataract of ignorance.

It is said that the ego lies in the head, which is why in the tradition of Sanatana Dharma one bows down to the Guru. Bowing down means, "I am surrendering my ego at Your feet, that Your Divine grace may flow down through them to wash away my burdensome ego." This is the attitude that one should have when one does prostration to the Guru. The only way to get rid of all the thoughts and all the confusion in the mind is to cultivate the attitude of true surrender.

We come to the spiritual master for our own benefit alone. The master has nothing to gain from us – it is totally the other way around.

Often, people do not understand the necessity of trying to surrender to a perfect Master. They ask, "Why is this necessary? Isn't it taking away our freedom?"

When people hear the word "surrender" they may feel that to surrender means bending down on their knees and offering everything that they have – and getting their bank balance down to zero. But Amma says that this is not true surrender. Real surrender is getting the inner bank balance to zero by offering everything that we have inside of us. True surrender is surrendering our hearts. By the act of bowing down we become uplifted.

There was once a great Sufi saint who lived in Northern India and who was known for fulfilling people's wishes. A poor old man who lived in a village needed to arrange his daughter's marriage but he had no money to do so. He had heard of the great saint and decided to make the journey to meet him.

When he reached the saint's abode, he approached him and asked if he could help to arrange for his daughter's marriage. The saint was very concerned and replied, "I don't have anything to give you now, but just give me 15 days and I will be able to arrange something for you." The old man left happily.

Fifteen days later, the man returned. He again approached the saint and reminded him of the promise to help him. This time the saint said, "Oh, it's you again. I completely forgot about it. If you can please come back in another 15 days I am sure I will be able to arrange something to help you." So the poor old man went off again.

Another 15 days passed by and on the destined day he again went to the saint to seek his help. He waited patiently for his turn and when he approached the saint once again, the saint said, "Oh, it's you. I again forgot about you. I am so sorry. I really don't have anything at all to offer you; all I have are these wooden sandals." He took off his pair of wooden sandals and gave them to the man. The poor old man was heart-broken, but quietly received them and turned to go on his way.

As he walked away, he sadly thought to himself, *Oh God, all I wanted was some help for my daughter's marriage, and look what this saint has given me: a pair of old wooden sandals. But it was my own fault, I should not have troubled him with my desires, he has nothing for himself even, so what could he give to me? Is it just my fate to suffer with poverty?*

Shedding silent tears, the man started to walk toward his village with the wooden sandals held against his heart.

At this time, a very wealthy man who happened to be one of the saint's most devoted disciples was making his way from another city. He was moving all of his businesses and his wealth to settle down at the feet of this great saint. He traveled on an elephant accompanied by a fleet of camels loaded with all his ancestral wealth.

As they started to approach the city, he suddenly noticed the fragrance of his Guru in the air. He could feel the divine presence somewhere nearby, so he stopped his elephant and started sniffing the air asking the people traveling with him, "Can you smell this fragrance? Where is it coming from?" His friends said they could not smell anything special, but the man insisted, "No, no, I feel as if my Master is somewhere nearby. I sense his divine essence."

He looked around and saw nobody except an old man walking slowly toward him in the distance. He told someone to call him. As the old man approached him the fragrance grew stronger and stronger. He asked the old man, "Where are you coming from? Where are you going? What is that you are carrying with you?"

The old man told his sad story and said, "I troubled that poor saint who didn't have anything, all he had to give me were his own wooden sandals." The disciple became very excited, "You are carrying my Guru's sandals? I must have them, what do you want in return for them?"

The old man was stunned and said, "I just wanted a bit of help to get my daughter married." The disciple immediately replied, "Take all of these camels laden with my wealth and immediately give me my Guru's sandals. They are the real wealth that I want!"

The old man answered, "But I don't need anything more than enough to get my daughter married."

Yet the disciple insisted, "No, you must take it all! I will not give you anything less for my Guru's sandals."

The old man handed over the sandals and the disciple placed them on top of his head and danced with ecstasy. He ran barefoot to the abode of his Master, where the saint was sitting as if waiting for him. The disciple prostrated to his Guru's feet, gently placing the slippers beneath them. The old saint smilingly asked him, "How much did you pay for them?"

With tears in his eyes, he said, "Master, whatever I had, all of my wealth, I gave to get these."

The Guru replied, "Even then, you got them very, very cheap!"

While we dream only of what we can get from life, perfect Masters like Amma dream only of what they can give to the world. Amma's desire is only to fill the world with love right up till the moment of Her last breath.

Amma explains that understanding the nature of the world and its objects and living accordingly is what it really means to surrender. People may become afraid when they hear the

word "surrender," so She suggests that we should use the word "acceptance" instead.

One day as a small group of people were out walking with Amma they saw the cast-off skin of a snake lying like a ribbon beside the path. One boy asked Amma, "Why do the snakes have to lose their skin?" Her reply was full of wisdom: "If the snakes do not shed their skin they cannot grow. They will suffocate in their old skin. Son, you also have to shed your old skin in order to grow."

In spiritual life there is no going backwards. Spiritual progress that we gain in life always remains. We may stop our practices and then start again after a long time, but that balance of our merit that we have achieved remains. Like having a savings account, when we add money the total amount increases, but the amount never diminishes and is never destroyed. Our endeavor to save is never wasted, and we can always start from that point again. From our part, we should develop the patience to put forth more and more effort in the right direction to help us experience the Truth.

A perfect Master teaches us to accept everything that happens in life. They help us to be thankful for both good and bad, right and wrong, enemy and friend, those who harm us and those who help us, those who cage us and those who release us from the cage. The Master helps us forget about the dark past and the bright future full of a thousand promises. The Master helps us live life in the present moment in all its fullness. They let us know that the whole of creation – everything, everybody, even our enemy – is helping us to evolve and attain perfection.

All great people have gone through extreme hardships in their lives. Galileo was one of the world's most renowned astronomers. He went blind but even in his darkest hour he could still say, "As it pleases God, it shall therefore please me also." He was so surrendered that he went on with his scientific experiments even after going blind.

Albert Einstein had a learning disability and did not speak until he was three years old. At school he found mathematics extremely challenging to study, but overcame this obstacle to become one of the world's greatest mathematicians.

George Washington also had a learning disability and was not gifted with writing or grammar skills. Despite these obvious stumbling blocks, he still triumphed over his weaknesses to become one of the greatest personalities in history.

In contemporary times, the scientist Stephen Hawking has managed to produce some of the most popular scientific literature the world has ever seen despite incredible physical limitations. Due to a debilitating disease he is confined to a wheelchair and is unable to speak or write. Even though his body is in this condition, he delves into unfolding the mysteries of the universe and has produced some of the most popular scientific literature used today.

Each of us will encounter difficulties along the spiritual path. Someone once asked Amma, "How should we strengthen our faith in bad times?" Amma replied,

> If you have real faith then you will not lose it. Only we ourselves gain from our faith in God. God has nothing to lose. When we have difficult times we should hold tightly to God's feet. When we love God we should not have expectations. Only through surrender will we be able to experience God. We have to go deep within. We have to

understand the thoughts in our mind, and look at where they are going to take us.

If we adopt spiritual principles in our lives, then no matter what situations we have to face, we will be able to deal with them in positive ways. In facing our challenges we will develop the strength to overcome any ordeal.

One day a partially deaf four-year-old boy came home from school with a note in his pocket from his teacher: "Your Tommy is too stupid to learn, get him out of the school." His mother read the callous note and answered the teacher, "He is not too stupid to learn. I will teach him myself." She immediately withdrew him from the school and with patience and discipline taught him herself at home. That young boy, thought to be unteachable, grew up with only three months of formal schooling. His full name was Thomas Alva Edison.

When the Guru says something, we should understand that it is for our ultimate good. Sometimes we may feel it does not sound logical, or is not really useful because it seems insignificant or does not make any sense. If Amma instructs us with spiritual advice or certain warnings, we should remember that if not for today, tomorrow it may have significance.

Amma once told us about a man that She felt had some heart problem. She suggested that he get himself checked by a doctor, but he refused as he felt that there was nothing wrong with him. Six months later he died of a heart attack.

On another occasion, Amma advised a different man that he should have his heart checked. He told Her that he had already done so in the UK, and that the doctors had not found anything wrong with him. Still Amma insisted that he should get his heart checked again. He did and this time they found that he actually had a triple block. When Amma says something, it is always for a reason.

The words of a Mahatma will always come true. So many times this has been proven in my life.

In the early days Amma always kept a close watch on the kitchen as She knew that it was probably the place dearest to us. She had said to me that even *I* would have to work in the kitchen one day. Well, that one day really did come.

All the ashram residents wanted to go and see Amma at Kodungallur, which was where Amma had installed the first *Brahmasthanam* temple, so everyone was excited to attend. The girl that usually cooked the ashram food for everybody really wanted to go to this program, so I volunteered to take over her job of cooking for one day to free her to go. I had never done any Indian cooking alone before, but it looked so easy. My menu was rice, spinach, and *pulisheri*.

I started out enthusiastically, but was amazed to discover how much spinach needed to be cut and then cooked to make a single serving, as all the bulk would cook down to almost nothing. I found myself spending a lot more time cutting up spinach than I had thought I would have to. The pulisheri was not too difficult, but I never managed to cook enough rice for everyone. I ended up having to cook rice four times that day to feed all the hungry construction workers as well as the residents.

At one point, my third batch of rice had finished cooking and was ready for draining. One of the *brahmacharis* wanted to help me drain it from the large steam cooker. He started to drain it from the big pot until suddenly he decided that it was getting too hot for him to hold. He cried out in alarm as he burnt his arm on the hot metal, dropping the whole pot of rice on the floor into the drain. Feeling very unsympathetic,

I chased him out of the kitchen and banned him from entering again to try and help me. I begrudgingly embarked upon cooking another batch of rice, after I had salvaged what I could.

After surviving the midday meal, the evening food distribution seemed a lot easier. A devotee had given the ashram some food that she had cooked at home. However, several extra people had shown up and once again the food turned out to be not quite enough to go around.

Another western girl was helping me with the distribution of the food and she could see that there was not enough for everyone. She insisted that we should take our share first. I told her that we could not do that, as the cooks should always go last, only taking if there was enough left over.

It turned out that there was not enough for everyone and this girl was not pleased that I had insisted that we eat last. We ended up going hungry. Later, she wrote me a letter thanking me for teaching her a lesson that day, which she had only come to appreciate afterward. Needless to say, I was elated when the cook returned to resume her work in the kitchen – I think everyone else was relieved also.

Well, Amma's words had come true. She had said I would have to cook the food one day, and lucky for everyone it was only for one day!

Chapter 4

Bridge to Freedom

*Just when the caterpillar thought the world
was over - it became a butterfly.*
                              Edward Teller

It is said that when the time is right, the spiritual master will come to us. We need not go searching for one. When we are ready for spiritual guidance, the master appears in our lives. For each person the first encounter is special and unique.

There are many interesting stories about how people have come to meet Amma for the first time. I heard of a man who was walking past a building in Sydney, Australia, where Amma's program was being held. He saw all the rows of shoes lined up and thought that there was a shoe sale going on, so he entered the building and went into the program place to try and buy a pair of shoes. When he found out that it was not a shoe sale he was a bit disappointed, but he took a pamphlet about Amma, put it in his pocket and left.

Later that day his wife was about to wash his clothes. Before putting them in the washing machine she first checked his pockets. She found the pamphlet about Amma, read it, and then became so curious about Amma that she decided to go and meet Her. She went to the program – and from then on became a devotee.

Another man brought his friend to see Amma. Both of them were disciples of Neem Karoli Baba who had died many years before. After receiving darshan the man asked his friend, "What do you think about Amma?"

The friend replied, "Well, She's okay, but She's not like our old master."

They sat down in the crowd a short distance from Amma. At that moment, Amma picked up a banana and threw it at them, which was the same exact thing that their old master was in the habit of doing. This person's opinion changed very quickly.

A woman wrote an email to me a short while ago telling me about some of her elderly friends that she had persuaded to come along with her to see Amma. These people reluctantly had agreed to come to the program, but later on were extremely grateful. Over cups of tea, they discussed what they had brought home from meeting Amma. The man, who was 89 years old, said that he found in Amma what he had been searching for his whole life...*real* love. And his 70-year-old wife admitted that finally she had found a sense of peace and contentment in her life. She had started regularly performing Amma's meditation technique, and proudly proclaimed that she had never missed a day of practice since she had learned it.

In New York, a woman related the story of how she had come to hear about Amma. She had met a homeless man who enthusiastically insisted that she must go and meet Amma and receive Her darshan. The homeless man's only possession had been his guitar and it had been stolen, which made him very upset. He went to see Amma, confided in Her his sorrow and amazingly got the guitar back. He was full of praise for Amma, telling people how wonderful She was. The woman told us this story, emphasizing how he had said she just *had* to come and see Amma.

Wherever Amma goes in the world, She reaches out to open people's hearts. She never forces anyone to come to Her, but spontaneously people are drawn. After some time they may start to discover the warmth of love beginning to grow within them. At a New York program all the big, rough-looking bouncers who worked at the program hall started to look a little mellower as the programs progressed. On the last day, one of them who was sitting on a chair watching Amma insisted, "You tell your boss She should stay at least one more week. We really need Her here!"

In Los Angeles, a hotel security guard spoke to me on the final day of the program. He was a little misty-eyed and said, "I am really going to miss you guys when you go; give me a hug." Being a monastic I dodged him quickly, replying that we would miss being there as well, and that *I* was not the one giving the hugs!

Every year before the U.S. tour, Amma usually gives all the residents of Amritapuri a personal darshan in Her room. In this encounter people get the chance to talk with Amma privately. For most people it is the highlight of the year to sit alone with Amma and talk about whatever they want, even if it is only for a few minutes. They long for this opportunity to be with Amma.

In 2006, I doubted that Amma would be able to conduct these private interviews for the ashram residents. That year we spent nine months of the year traveling. We made our way from the southern end of India to the north, driving across

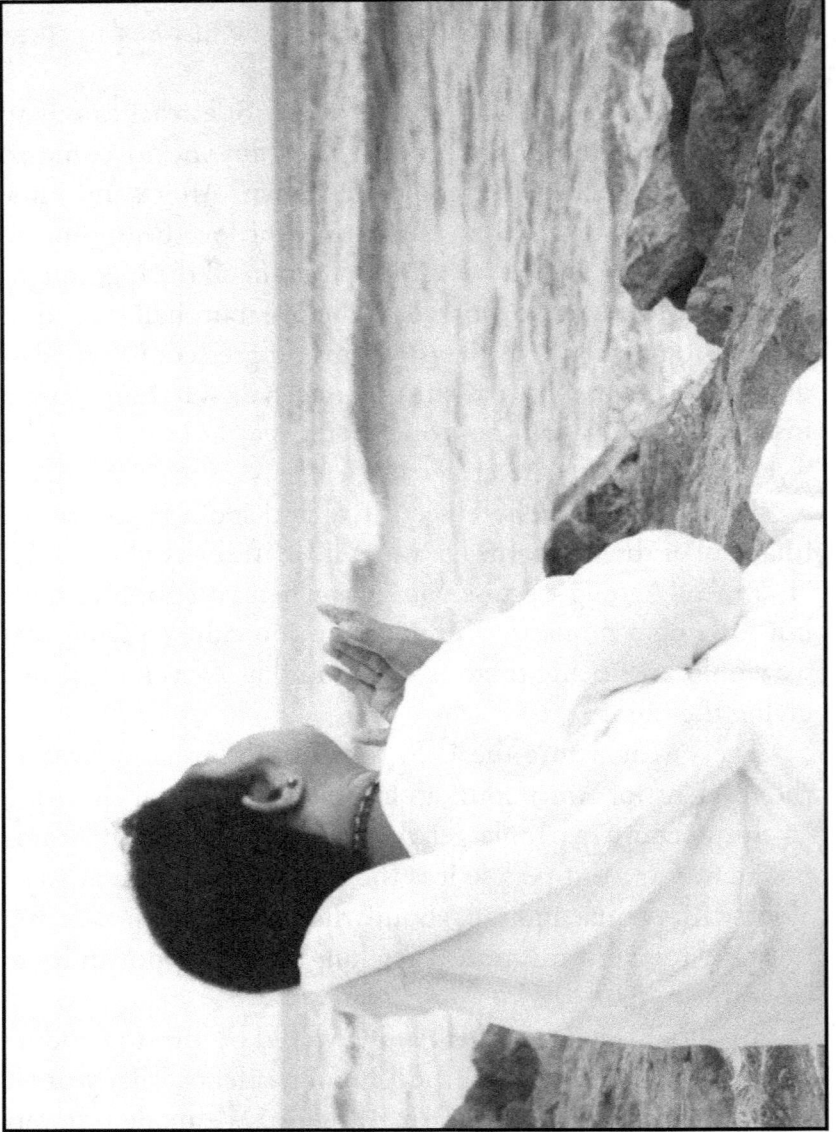

bumpy roads for two months, a caravan of seven buses and various other vehicles. We then made our way from North India to Australia, Singapore and Malaysia. We returned to the ashram only for three days before going to New York for a two-day event. The very same night that we returned to India, Amma conducted a large public program. Some people may worry about experiencing jet-lag, but we do not have the time to even think about this! We then continued on another circuit of programs throughout South India. Amma was at the Amritapuri ashram only a few days before starting off for the U.S. tour. We ended up spending a mere two weeks out of the first half of the year in the ashram.

Our travel schedule had kept us out of the ashram for such a long period of time that I could not imagine how Amma could hold all those private darshans in Her room in only four days. As there are more than 3,000 residents in the ashram, it seemed impossible that She could make the time to see everyone, so I thought for sure that She would postpone these darshans. When people asked me, I told them not to expect to see Amma alone until later in the year. How would it be possible to see everyone in just a few days? But the next thing I knew, Amma had already started giving the room darshans.

In Her own characteristic way, She began the darshans in the late hours of the night after returning from public programs where She had given darshan to at least 100,000 people.

She stayed up all night seeing everyone individually. Amma is accustomed to staying up all night, but this was something that She was doing in Her *free* time. After having met with all the residents, Amma still managed to give darshan to the ones staying at different ashram branches, people working at Her schools as well as many of the devotees that work at the *AIMS* hospital and other institutions.

To top this all off, I was shocked to hear that Amma had suddenly called for a public darshan day on the day before we were to leave for the U.S. tour. Once you invite thousands of people for the day, it is very hard to get them to leave straight away. I thought this was really just too much, but Amma was happy for another chance to give Her absolute maximum. On what was supposed to be a rest day before traveling, She sat through a 15-hour stretch giving darshan. The program finished in the early morning hours and we left for the airport that same afternoon. As usual, wherever we go, even at the airport there was another darshan session for Amma.

Traveling transit through Sri Lanka, while some of us were finally catching up on rest, Amma spent most of Her time with the brahmacharis who were building the tsunami relief houses for the people there. Amma guided them in their work and gave them a chance to spend time with Her like everyone else had just received. It amazes me that Amma still continues to give so much of Herself to everyone, to Her utmost capacity, no matter how busy Her schedule is.

On the way to the U.S., we had a three-day program in Japan. Amma mentioned several times how tired She was and that She could not understand why. I myself had a very good idea why She might be feeling exhausted!

After talking with one of the girls who had flown from the U.S. to join the program in Japan, I suddenly had a brilliant idea. This girl had told me how she had seen how the comfortable seats in the First Class section of the plane reclined all the way down flat. Knowing how Amma is never really able to sleep properly on the plane, I thought that perhaps we could use our frequent flier miles and upgrade to First Class so that She would be able to catch up on some rest. The few people that I mentioned this to thought it was a great idea, so we went ahead with the plan and upgraded three seats to First Class.

I was ready with several excuses to justify this upgrade. We would never have the chance to use the miles, we needed the extra luggage allowance and Amma could really rest well on the flight. When I went up to Amma to break the good news to Her about what I had arranged, Amma clearly stated Her reaction to this change in a few words. She firmly replied, *"Amma is NOT going to get on that plane if She is in First Class!"*

After my initial shock, I hate to admit it but for a few seconds as I was walking away from Amma, a little voice rose up inside of me saying, *Well let's just see whose will is stronger!* It was a really stupid thought to have considering that I was dealing with Amma.

I reported back to the person arranging our travel bookings and conveyed Amma's message. As it was late at night and we were due to leave the next afternoon, we decided that it was too late to do anything at that point so we would have to wait until our arrival in the airport the next day. Thinking that Amma surely was not serious about what She had said, we were secretly hoping that it would be too late to change again and we would simply *have* to be stuck comfortably in First Class for the flight.

The next day when we arrived at the airport I went over to the counter to start our check-in procedure, with the hope that Amma would have forgotten all about the previous night. We had all the large heavy suitcases lined up ready to be checked-in. I went over to where Amma was giving a final darshan to the devotees and asked Her to come to the counter so that we could finish the procedure.

Amma emphatically reminded me that She was *not* getting on that plane if She was in First Class. I started to sweat a little seeing the trouble that I was in now. However, I noticed a few very happy devotees who were staying at the Japanese ashram – they were thrilled at the thought of Amma staying with them a little while longer. I rushed back to the counter to plead with the lady that I had made a big mistake and could we please downgrade now? I was worried that all the devotees in America would kill me if Amma did not turn up in time for the first program.

Luckily we were able to downgrade. I hurried back to tell Amma that we were not in First Class anymore, so could She please come over to the counter and check-in? Amma graciously agreed and proceeded to the counter.

Half an hour later, Amma quietly explained to me that She *had* to set an example for us. If She traveled in luxury, then other people in the ashram who look to Her as an example would want to do this too. The way Amma lives Her life and performs Her actions always sets a perfect example for us.

While being interviewed by the press, Amma was asked this question: "Amma has become so successful. How does She do it?"

Amma answered, "First of all, one must set an example. If you are setting an example in a very genuine way then others will follow, but you have to be spontaneous."

Someone shared with me some of the precious words that Amma had said to her one day when she felt sad. Amma said that She travels by road sometimes just to save a few dollars. She has seen so much suffering in Her life. She said that She sits at times for 20 hours a day giving darshan, sitting in the mud with all of us trying to pull us out. We are like flowers covered in mud and She is patiently cleaning all the flowers. Some flowers are very beautiful. Amma told this girl that she is a beautiful flower and that She has spent a lot of time cleaning her with great care since early in her childhood. She has done this so that she can set an example and reflect Amma's message to the world.

Amma said these flowers are very valuable, but not knowing their value or thinking themselves to be worthless, they throw themselves back into the mud. However, Amma patiently pulls us out of the mud again and again, and tries to clean us. Out of Her infinite compassion, Amma comes to us to uplift and strengthen us. She could choose to remain in an exalted state of bliss, but She wishes instead to sacrifice Herself for the sake of humanity.

Chapter 5

Humility in Simplicity

If you get to thinking you are a person of some influence, try ordering someone else's dog around.
                                                                    Internet Proverb

During the Amritavarsham50 celebrations in Cochin in 2003, there were four days of events scheduled. On the final day, just before the main event, we walked onto the stage and Amma looked at the chair that had been beautifully decorated for Her to sit on. She said to me, "Remove the cloth." She did not like the look of it as it had a little gold work on the edges, and She thought it was too fancy. On numerous occasions Amma had always stressed that She prefers simple cloth to be used for Her, as it saves money and also sets the example of simplicity for others. Since hundreds of thousands of people were watching me, I was horrified at the thought that I would have to tear the chair apart and try to find a plain cloth for it, all in the next few seconds!

"Amma *please*, it is only just a *tiny* bit of gold on the sides of it!" I begged.

Luckily for me, Amma compassionately realized the situation I would be in if I had to try to find something else to cover the chair with at the last minute, so She reluctantly agreed to sit on the chair. I was so relieved. No matter where we are or what situation we are in, Amma insists on making Her teachings quite clear by Her personal example.

Humility is the quality we most need in order to find peace and harmony in the world. Only when we become humble within, can there be harmony on the outside.

The wars and violence that we see today have all started from the mind. A thought emerges from the mind and then is put later into action. Then that action may expand to cause an incredible amount of violence. Before we can exhaust all the negativities inside of us and before we can truly become compassionate, we must first have the attitude of humility.

The ego follows us like a shadow. But when our forehead is on the ground there is no shadow. Humility is the sword that can cut down the ego, the selfishness in us. We cannot get rid of the ego completely; it is there in everyone. Still, if we put forth effort with an innocent attitude, divine grace will certainly flow to us and some of the ego can be washed away.

We cannot destroy the ego on our own. We need the guidance of a spiritual Master in order to attain the kind of humility needed to transcend the ego and vasanas. If we have the right outlook, wherever we may be in the world, grace from the Master can flow to us to help us overcome our vasanas. We do not necessarily have to be in their physical presence to experience this grace.

When our ego begins to melt away, we start to become humble. This humility will enable us to receive grace. We will then be able to understand the deeper meaning behind each of the Guru's actions and words. This is why Amma says we need the quality of humility. We should have the perspective of a beginner to really understand the deeper meaning behind what the Guru says and does.

The greatest beings in this world have always been the humblest and simplest. Research was done into the most successful companies and the CEOs that guided these companies to the top ranks of the business world. Contrary to all expectations, it was found that the most successful managers were actually very quiet and reserved, often even shy. They were not egotistical, but sincere, ordinary people who worked extremely hard.

When the leaders from less successful, lower-ranked companies were compared with them, it was found that most of them had enormous egos. The administrators of the smaller companies wanted to take all the credit for any success, yet blamed others when their companies performed poorly.

In comparison, the humble leaders were always ready to attribute their good fortune to factors other than themselves and when things did not go well, they took full responsibility for the mistakes.

Amma has become one of the greatest examples of the triumph of humility. Coming from a simple background with little formal education, She has risen up in the world to become one of its greatest CEOs. The globally acclaimed leader of an ever-expanding service organization. She is the ultimate CEO, guiding thousands of people in humanitarian work with a vast amount of compassion, humility, patience and sincerity. She has no need to be appreciated or congratulated about Her achievements, but only desires to serve humanity, relieve suffering, uplift the poor and inspire us all to lead a good life.

Amma has often been asked if She would ever consider going into politics. She usually laughs and replies that She has no desire to be the head of anything. She wants only to be the sweeper, sweeping our minds, sweeping away suffering and poverty and serving the world. While most of us are busy building ourselves up, Amma reminds us of the importance of practicing humility. Her unassuming nature is so genuine that we are inspired to join in the sweeping and stop worrying about trying to get ahead.

Amma never sees any task as being beneath Her. Her overwhelming humility often leads Her to become the first one to participate in any job that others might be reluctant to perform.

After a two-day program in Durgapur in 2004, we were leaving the program site to travel by road to Calcutta. Amma asked one of the brahmacharis if the site from the program had been cleaned. He answered that it had, but as we were driving out Amma noticed that there were still lots of leaf plates and papers on the ground. She stopped the car, got out, and started cleaning up the rubbish. Of course this quickly inspired the 500 people traveling with the tour to join in the task. With everyone's help the field was quickly cleaned and the rubbish was hastily burned up. Amma is never shy to start people in performing the right action when the need is there.

Most recently in 2007, near the end of a program in Tamil Nadu, Amma insisted that the people traveling with Her go out and clean the grounds and help to dismantle the temporary structures that had been specially built for the program. The devotees were happy to do this, and completely surprised when the police who were on duty for the program also joined in with the work. It was an amazing sight to see. Amma has the capacity to inspire everyone to want to help do something good, no matter who they may be.

The police had never before joined in with our work, but these officers had been so profoundly touched by Amma and impressed with how hard everyone worked that they wanted to do something to help as well. We often see the police force as people that are very different from us because they have a completely different role to play. But in front of Amma all differences disappear and merge in Her motherly love.

At the end of a public program in Chennai, two policewomen followed Amma to a house visit. They asked Amma if they could speak with Her privately for a few minutes. One of them started to unburden her heart to Amma. Slowly tears formed in her eyes. She told the sad story of having been pregnant once and then having miscarried. She became pregnant again, but at five months was hit from behind by a bus and again miscarried. Now she was having difficulty conceiving and wanted Amma to bless her for this. Amma gently wiped away the woman's tears and then Her own, and promised to make a *sankalpa* for her.

The second policewoman then had her turn to tell her problems to Amma. She had a lot of family problems, among them that her husband often beat her. She was so sad and depressed that she was contemplating suicide. Amma embraced Her, making her promise that she would never do this and offered her some advice to help with the situation. When the two policewomen had finished speaking to Amma, both of them dried their tears with handkerchiefs, stepped back a few steps and let the next people come into the room to tell their own problems as well. After a few deep breaths to gain control over their emotions again, the policewomen left the room.

When we were leaving the house, one of the women took my arm and quietly said a very grateful thank-you to me. I had done nothing; I was simply standing close by Amma, the silent witness in the wake of Her overflowing, compassionate love.

After having seen these women and the police that helped at the program earlier, my perspective of the police really changed. I no longer saw them as just a uniform. I now understood them to be people who want and need a mother's love and someone to confide their problems to, just like the rest of us.

Even though Amma has nothing more to gain in this world, and no one would ever question Her right to take rest, She never sits idle. When She is not giving darshan, for most of the day She reads each and every letter that is given to Her. In Her spare time She gives guidance to those in need, as well as to the people supervising the institutions that are run in Her name.

Amma has thousands of people working all over the world performing service activities for Her. Though they very enthusiastically do the work, they often lack experience in dealing with practical matters, so Amma has to regularly advise them. Some may think that when Amma is not conducting programs or giving darshan that She is taking rest, but Her time is usually spent meeting with people to guide them on the next course of action or directing them over the phone. Rarely does She actually take any rest.

When we arrive at programs in India, I usually follow Amma out of the car on Her side, because the crowds are very excitable and it is good for me to be next to Her straight away to protect Her. (Actually I need to be close to Amma so She can protect me!) It may look as if I am holding onto Amma so that She will not fall, but in truth it is really the other way around. I am holding onto Her so that I do not fall, both literally and figuratively.

One evening we arrived in Trivandrum for a program. Devotees had enthusiastically placed garlands on Amma through the windows of the car, as we slowly drove through

the narrow lane before reaching the Trivandrum ashram. Garlands filled the car. When we arrived, Amma picked up a few of the flower garlands that were on the floor by Her feet and put them on the seat with all of the other ones, then moved them all together. I was watching Her re-arrange them and wondering what She was doing, as there was a seething mass of people awaiting Her.

As I got out of the car, I finally realized that Amma had re-arranged them so that I would have space to move over the seat to come behind Her. I could have moved them quite easily myself, but Amma took the time and trouble to move the garlands for me. I felt humbled by Amma's gesture of consideration. It is supposed to be that the disciple serves the Guru, but with Amma it is really the other way around – She is always serving us.

After we got out of the car, we walked along the pathway lined with wooden benches that had large, lighted oil lamps placed on top of them. The crowd stood behind the benches. But this was not a very good plan because the people could not help but push forward straining to touch Amma.

She told everyone all along the way to be careful of the oil lamps and warned them not to rush forward due to the dangerous situation. She went to the trouble of making sure that the people behind each and every oil lamp were safe from being burned, and insisted that they were careful not to push each other into them.

At the end of the line, a large crush of people waited inside the building for Amma to enter. In all the excitement, the devotee who was supposed to perform the arati to Amma could not get the camphor lit. Amma, the ever-helpful and considerate mother, patiently took the time to light the camphor Herself, so the devotee could complete the traditional ceremony.

Amma is always concerned that everyone is taken care of. Whenever She appears at a program, She first looks around to make sure that all have a reasonable place to sit. She does not want people to have to sit in the rain or sun. She may ask for barricades or signboards that are blocking people's view to be taken down. The men filming will often be told to sit down so that everyone can see.

Amma will always put the needs of others first. At the beginning of the satsang She may apologize for not having enough space for everyone to sit. Instead of aiming to show the greatness of a wise orator, Amma exemplifies the never-ending flow of a compassionate mother. Amma is able to do many things at once. Even as She is receiving the crowds during darshan, She still focuses on the needs of those who are waiting, making sure that they are served water or that they do not have to stand in the sun if it can be helped. She also often announces over the sound system that people should be careful of their jewelry and valuables, to assure nothing is stolen by thieves that may be lurking in the large crowds.

Practicality helps us get through difficulties in spiritual life. Amma teaches this to us through everyday examples. Once Amma was giving darshan and a person was sick and about to vomit, so Amma emptied out the *prasad* plate next to Her and gave it to the person so he could throw up into it. She never considered it to be too holy as we might have. Amma is always totally practical and thoughtful of others.

A true Master will never ask us to give up everything, but instead teaches us to take just enough for our own needs. Amma tries to teach us to share and to open up our hearts with others. This attitude of sharing makes us become more compassionate and truly speeds up our spiritual growth. All spiritual practices are meant to help us awaken the love that lies inside of us. Even people who do not perform traditional spiritual practices but have learned to share, will experience some peace by their selfless attitude.

On one occasion we were waiting in an airline lounge for our flight to start boarding and I had given Amma some tea to drink. She then told me to give tea to the *swamis* who were waiting in another area. I remarked that someone surely would have given them tea already, but Amma insisted I should take it for them. She wanted to instill in me the idea of thinking of others before oneself in every situation. Amma does not think of Her own needs, but always puts others first. No matter how busy She is, She will constantly think of others before Herself. Her whole life is dedicated as an offering to serve the world.

There is a true story that illustrates the value of considering the needs of others. A group of about 70 scientists worked very hard for 12 to 18 hours every day at a rocket launching station. As the launch-date neared, they grew increasingly frustrated due to the pressure of their intense schedule. Their boss worked them hard, but they all felt very loyal to him and never thought of quitting the job.

One morning, one of the scientists went to the boss and told him that he had promised to take his children to an exhibition that had come to town. He asked for permission to leave the office at 5:30 p.m. to be able to do this. His boss agreed. The scientist started his work and became very concentrated throughout the day. He finally checked his watch, as he thought it was about time for him to leave and was shocked to see that it was already 8:30 p.m.

Disappointed that he had missed his chance to take his children to the exhibition, he searched for his boss to let him know that he was leaving. He could not find him anywhere. He felt very guilty for missing the chance to be with his children when they had so eagerly been looking forward to it.

When he reached home it was very quiet and his children were not to be seen. He found his wife working in the kitchen and very gingerly approached her, thinking that she would be extremely angry with him. To his surprise she smiled pleasantly. He dared to ask her where the children were. It was her turn to be surprised. She replied that his boss had come at 5:15 p.m. and had taken the children to the exhibition.

It turned out that his boss had come by the scientist's office at 5:00 p.m. When his boss saw him so deeply engrossed in his work, he knew that it would be difficult for him to disengage at that time. Feeling that the children should not miss out on the exhibition, his boss decided to take them to see it himself. The couple was very happy to realize what a kind, considerate and extremely intelligent boss the husband had.

This incident occurred some years before the thoughtful boss became the President of India: Dr. A. P. J. Abdul Kalam.

Most of our life is spent in performing actions for our own sake. We so rarely take the time to think of others. Most of us spend our lives being busy all the time, but rarely achieve anything meaningful at all. Amma inspires us to try to go beyond our selfishness and become truly selfless in our thoughts and our actions.

Chapter 6

What is Real Happiness?

*Praise and blame, gain and loss, pleasure and
sorrow - all come and go like the wind. To be happy,
rest like a giant tree in the midst of them all.*
The Buddha

In days gone by, the King of Spain once said, "I have ruled for 50 years in victory and peace. Beloved by my subjects, dreaded by my enemies and respected by my allies. Riches and honors, power and pleasure, have all waited on my call. No earthly blessing appears to have been wanting my felicity. Yet, I have diligently counted the days of pure and genuine happiness and strangely enough, they amount to… only 14…"

Like this king, people search their whole lives trying to find the best of everything. Even when we obtain all that we desire, we will not necessarily be happy.

One time when we stayed in a luxury hotel in the U.S. for a retreat, there were five pillows on each bed. I wanted to sleep on the floor so was searching in the drawer for a blanket, which I found eventually. But in the top drawer do you know what I found? Another pillow! I could not believe that five pillows might not be enough for someone. If we believe that we need certain things from life in order to feel satisfied, then we will never be content.

I read of an interview with a famous celebrity who said: "We all have in common the feeling of being out of balance. Most people have an ardent desire to be happy and peaceful but very few among us attain that state. No person or possession will bring us this state of inner calm… the only thing that can fill that emptiness is a higher power. I am convinced that there is a superior being above us. If we were left up to ourselves, we would be destined to chaos."

We are so fortunate to have a spiritual guide like Amma who can show us where true happiness lies.

Amma often says that in today's world, everyone wants to be a king on the outside – but on the inside, we remain simply beggars. If we keep begging, we will die as a beggar; but when we learn to give, we become like a king. We should try to transform ourselves from beggars to kings – on the inside, not just on the outside.

The joy that we get in the company of a Saint is not the joy that the Saint gives us, but that which manifests from inside our own heart. It is just like the lotus bud that opens up and blossoms beautifully, giving out its fragrance at dawn. The sun is only an apparent cause for the bud to flower. Nothing new that was not already inherent in the bud comes out. Similarly, in the presence of an enlightened soul, the hidden joy within us reveals itself.

Love is very much hidden within the hearts of everyone. Amma often tells that we should try to see the good in everything, as even the lotus flowers bloom from the mud and filth of dirty water. When we become full of compassion, then we start to see everyone else as a part of our own Self, and in this state our heart begins to overflow with love.

It is guaranteed that one who does not know the nature of life will suffer a lot of pain. But someone who knows the nature of the world can accept anything that happens with a smile, and nothing adversely affects them. If we try only to gain external things, we will be unhappy whether we receive them or not. Happiness can never be found from something external. It has to come from within.

A 92-year-old man with ailing vision had to move to a nursing home because his wife of 70 years had recently passed away. The petite, proud man was always fully dressed each morning by eight o'clock, freshly shaved, with his hair neatly combed. On the day of his move, he sat in the lobby of the nursing home patiently waiting to be shown to his new room. He smiled sweetly when the attendant told him that his room was ready. As he maneuvered his walker to the elevator, the attendant provided a visual description of his tiny room, including the furniture and the color of the curtains that had been hung on his window. "I love it," he stated with the enthusiasm of an eight-year-old having just been presented with a new puppy.

"Mr. Smith, you haven't even seen the room yet; just wait."

"That doesn't have anything to do with it," he replied. "Happiness is something you decide on ahead of time. Whether I like my room or not doesn't depend on how the furniture is arranged – it's how I arrange my mind. I already decided to love it. It's a decision I make every morning when I wake up. I have a choice; I can spend the day in bed recounting the difficulty I have with the parts of my body that no longer work, or get out of bed and be thankful for the ones that do. Each day is a gift and as long as my eyes open, I'll focus on the new day and all the happy memories I've stored away just for this time in my life."

Despite all the knowledge, wealth and achievements that we might acquire in life, if we do not have any concern for the welfare of the world, then everything we have acquired becomes useless. However, this does not mean that we should not try to do anything in life.

One girl told me that she was confused for a long time after hearing some spiritual teachings about the futility of material pursuits. She had stopped doing the things that she had always loved to do so much, like writing poetry and painting, but she eventually had her doubts cleared. Amma told her that creativity is not an obstacle to spiritual life. We can do anything that we really want to do, but we should just keep at the back of our mind the knowledge that nothing in this whole outside world is going to make us happy.

One of the brahmacharis stationed at a branch ashram in Northern India, related his experiences of recently traveling to the Himalayas. He had been quite happy staying at the ashram branch, but felt that his mind was strong enough to be able to go off to a forest in the Himalayas to meditate and perform *tapas*. After reaching the forest he found that this was not the case; he did not find any stillness of mind there at all. Instead, so many other feelings and thoughts started to arise in his mind and he even became quite fearful. He left the forest to stay among the other yogis in the foothills, thinking this would improve his situation.

When he saw how some of the people lived there, his concept of spiritual life in the Himalayas was dashed to pieces. The *sadhus* took their meals at 7:00 a.m. in the morning, and again at 4:00 p.m. in the afternoon. They ate to their fill, and

then slept after a good meal. They sat around smoking *beedies* or *chillums* and talking of Vedanta. Some of them even ended up fighting with each other because they disagreed on some point. The brahmachari said that he never came across anyone talking devotionally about God, and not one of the yogis acted lovingly with others. People often avoided each other as they were afraid that they might have to show some hospitality and offer a cup of tea, thereby cutting down on their monetary resources.

His experiences reflect what Amma often says about Vedanta: that we should not just talk about it, but instead we should actually try to live it.

The mind can never be still; there will always be thoughts that will come to disturb us. The mind will follow us wherever we go, from the heights of the Himalayas to the depths of the deepest forests. It will always plague us – there is no escape. Amma advises that it is better to do some work for the world, instead of trying only to still the mind. The brahmachari remarked that he felt much happier now that he was doing some service work again. He found that people around Amma were much more selfless than most of the yogis that he had met living in the Himalayas.

The great philosopher Aristotle was asked a question by a group of his students: "Master, you have taught for decades and have written many books. Tell us in a few words, what is the purpose of knowledge?"

Aristotle answered them, "The meaning, the purpose of knowledge, is in one single thought – service."

Just a few months ago I overheard Amma talking to a guest who was visiting the ashram in India. She said,

I do not mind if my children want to spend all their time meditating, or if they only want to work hard, as long as they should not be lazy. They can work hard if they want to and if they want to meditate, let them spend at least a little time working every day so that they make enough money for the food that they take. And then let them work a little bit more so that they can make ten rupees that can be used to serve the world. That is all I ask of any one. They should not depend on others for their existence.

Even if we feel we cannot fit in with all the spiritual practices, at least we can work hard at doing something, because that is all that Amma expects from us. There is no one that does not fit in with Her. She accepts everyone.

A special Japanese boy traveled to India with a group of 80 students that annually helps to build free houses for the poor. This boy suffered from cerebral palsy, and with his crippled body was mostly confined to a wheelchair. He had an intense desire to contribute like all the other students, especially because the houses were intended for the tsunami victims. Regrettably, most of the work required difficult manual labor that was impossible for him to do, such as moving heavy building supplies.

Finally a solution was found. Wearing a glove on his one good hand, a paintbrush was tied to it and he was able to move his arm well enough to paint the walls of the houses. Although just as much paint was splashed over him and everywhere else, as went on the walls, no one minded. Even with the intense sun relentlessly beating down on him, he did not care – he was happy.

He later said, "You know, my whole life I have always had other people serving me. At last I have found something to do to help someone else. I feel that if Amma was in my body, then She would want to work hard like this also." He was so thrilled to be able to help at last.

Our happiness lies in the happiness of others. Some people think that by exploiting others they can be happy, but this is not true. Only by trying to be useful to others, by sacrificing our own interest for their sake, can we find true happiness. If we can do something with love in our heart and undergo sacrifice for the sake of others, we will experience peace and joy. Whatever work we engage in for the good of humanity will make our life blessed.

Chapter 7

The Power of Love

*The reason two antelope walk together, is so that
one can blow the dust out of the eyes of the other.*
African proverb

The love between the Guru and the disciple is the purest
kind of love that can ever be experienced in this world.
This love is so profound because the Guru simply loves, not
expecting anything in return. The Guru's only expectation is
to take the disciple to the realm of the Supreme Truth through
the path of grace.

Other kinds of love experienced in the world are rarely of
this quality. The love that most of us have known is conditional,
often based on hidden expectations, and usually met with disap-
pointment. Even an innocent baby loves its mother in the hope
that it will receive nourishing breast milk. Everyone's love has
a price tag attached to it. But Amma feels there should be one
place in the world where there is selfless love without any price
attached, without any expectation. That is why She has come.

At an evening program on the U.S. tour, the translator
asked Amma if She wanted Her usual teachings about love to
be translated. Amma stated, "Yes," that it should be done. She
laughed, as She sensed that the translator was a little tired of

having to repeat all of the same teachings about love day after day. Amma said that She never, ever tires of talking about love. For Her the topic of love is always fresh and new, because She experiences the fullness of it all the time. Love is not just a word for Her but an ever-exciting experience. She told the translator that he should never underestimate the power of love, which is something that unfortunately most of us often do.

The power of love, the power of the soul, exists within everyone. It is Amma's quest to awaken that potential of infinite power: the motherhood in people – both men and women; the love and compassion in everyone. Pure love has the capacity to create tremendous change in each of us and in the world.

A woman journalist researching a story about animals was amazed to meet a former female heroin addict, who had fallen in love with a stray dog. The addict realized that she would have to clean herself up in order to be able to properly care for the animal. She took the responsibility to reform herself and gave up drugs, so she could competently care for her pet. She saved the dog and the dog rescued her.

Journalists often ask Amma to describe what it is like to embrace the people that come to Her. Amma answers them, "It is a very pure experience. I see in people a reflection of myself. When I look at the people I become them and feel their sorrows and joys. We meet at the level of love."

When Amma gives darshan, She acts as a catalyst to help us experience our deepest true nature. We have been drinking ditch water for so long that when we come into contact with pure water, it is so wonderfully refreshing. We get a glimpse of our own inner Divine nature in Amma.

Amma says that She is not just confined to Her five foot tall body. She says that if you look within yourself, you will find Her residing in your heart. She resides as the internal Self hidden within each person. It is because we do not have awareness of this experience that we feel Amma is not with us all the time. Each and every moment She is with us and closest to us – She is our very own Self.

Most of us only think about material gains and losses but the greatest gain that we can have in life is love. All the different spiritual practices that we do are actually intended to awaken the dormant essence of love lying inside of us, just underneath the surface of our likes and dislikes.

Just as a spider that spins its web can get caught up in it, we also can get entangled in the web of desires that we weave. We become enclosed in our own private little universe based on *maya*. Only an enlightened soul can pull us out of this tangled web of our own creation.

There was once a man who had a great deal of love for Amma. But Amma could see what no one else could – that inside he carried a heavy burden of deep wounds from the past. She knew something was always troubling him. He confided to Amma that one of his children had committed suicide a long time ago and he could never forget it. Yet simply by loving Amma, this wound from the past was unimaginably healed. She advised him to forget the past as it was all a cancelled check. Like the doctor who prescribes medicine to cure the patient's illness, Amma offers each of us exactly what we need to heal our hearts.

Amma loves all beings equally in this creation. One night in the ashram, Amma had an uncomfortable feeling that something was wrong with one of the cows. She felt that maybe they had not been fed properly and that one of them might be hungry. She phoned up the brahmachari in charge of the cowshed and asked him if all the cows had been fed. He replied that they had. Still Amma was feeling that something was wrong and so She went to investigate.

Arriving at the cowshed, She filled a container with cow food and put it in front of one of the calves. The calf ate everything. Seeing how hungry the calf was, Amma inquired about this. The brahmachari suddenly remembered that this calf's mother had died and another brahmachari was put in charge of only this one. However, he had gone off for the day and everyone else had forgotten to feed it. But not Amma – She knew of the calf's hunger without being told.

Amma says that in the olden days, mothers had such a deep bond of love with their children that even if the child was far away, the mother's breast would start to leak milk when the child was hungry, so she knew spontaneously that it was time to feed the child. Nowadays, the bond of love is not as strong. People even have to call the mother on a cell phone to let her know that her child is hungry.

The world is filled with selfishness. People give love with expectations because they have not realized where the very source of love lies. We are always searching to gain something from the outside but vain attempts only leave us sorrowful, unfulfilled and empty. Seeing so many people suffering in this manner, Amma feels immense compassion and tries to bring us out of this state.

Someone once asked Amma, "How can I love myself more?" Amma answered, "If we love others and develop good qualities, we will be able to love ourselves." She suggests that even if we are not able to love others, at least we should try not to be angry towards them. We should try not to have hatred towards anybody, even though it may be difficult.

It is easy to love Amma, but we must try to show that same love we feel for Her to other people. If we cannot feel love for someone, then we have usually misunderstood them. It is easier to love others when we try to comprehend the unfortunate circumstances that people may have come from.

Amma says that once we really understand and imbibe the true essence of spirituality properly, then compassion, love and concern for others will start to arise in us. Only when we start loving, will we be able to feel and experience real love.

At a question and answer session with Amma, I felt that the questioner was being slightly rude, alluding to the fact that Amma used a translator and suggesting that Amma should know English fluently. I was a little disturbed by the question but Amma was not fazed at all. She never is.

The question was, "If Amma is omniscient, shouldn't She be able to understand every language?"

Amma's answer was wonderful. She immediately replied, "Omniscience means understanding knowledge about what is eternal, and in that plane of consciousness, the language is love."

Nothing needed to be said after that.

While we were in Spain on the 2006 European tour, we saw a young boy with Down syndrome who had learned to play the *tabla* in Amritapuri. Amma was happy to see him again. She invited him to come to the stage during the evening program and play tabla during Her *bhajans*.

It was stunning to see this young boy playing near Amma. Although many accomplished artists have attended Amma's programs, they have rarely been invited to play music with Her, but on two different occasions, Amma lovingly invited this boy to accompany Her bhajans. Almost every song, Amma turned around to smile at him with encouragement. He beamed back at Her. During the meditation at the end of the program, She gestured for him to join Her sitting on the *peetham*. After this, Amma made him walk in front of Her through the crowd toward Her chair. Although he could not understand Her language, he could always comprehend exactly what Amma asked him to do. With the communication of love, understanding of the words is not needed. A mother's heart can always be understood by her children.

Amma is fluent in the language of love and She is trying to teach it to us as well.

We are often reminded not to fall in love, which usually ends up only being infatuation, but to *become* love. It is love that makes us fearless, outspoken and powerful, and utterly free. People have done many incredible things for the sake of love. Infinite power and potential is tapped into and drawn forth because of this love.

In 2002, a famous American celebrity asked the South African President Nelson Mandela what he wanted as a gift for his nation. He answered simply, "Build me a school." Within several years a multi-million dollar structure arose from the dry soil in Soweto, a poor town near Johannesburg. A school for disadvantaged girls was built as a gift of love. The seeds of a new generation had been planted.

The founder of the school came from a poor, oppressed background, which is why she wanted to give the younger generation a chance to escape that misfortune. She wanted to give them all that she never had while growing up, because she knew these young people would be the leaders of tomorrow's world. Her gift of love benefited so many young people, and has made her feel with joy that her life has come full circle. People often ask her why she never had children of her own.

She answers, that in discovering this selfless love within, she has realized that she does not need to have her own children but instead can help to bring up other people's children.

There is a story of a Japanese man who had a powerful revelation while he was renovating a small house. When he was tearing down one of the walls, he found a lizard with a nail driven through its foot. On closer examination of the nail, the man could see that it was probably from ten years before when the house had initially been constructed, as no work had been done on the house since then. Wondering how a lizard could survive for so long without moving, the man sat in contemplation watching the poor lizard. He could not imagine how it had managed to get food for all those years. Lo and behold, another lizard appeared with food in its mouth and offered it to the trapped lizard. Shocked, the man realized that this second lizard had probably been feeding its mate for ten years. That, he realized, was the power of love.

When the top floors of the temple building in Amritapuri were being completed, the ashram residents participated in brick *seva* to help finish the construction work. We assisted the workers by bringing all of the supplies to them, which meant that we carried bricks and other building supplies up several flights of stairs.

Normally, when we walked up the stairs just carrying ourselves, we had to stop part way to catch our breath, wondering if we could find the strength to reach the top. But during the brick seva we were able to carry at least a couple of heavy bricks up the flights of stairs repeatedly for a few hours. It was a miracle of Amma's grace that we found the strength to carry this weight up the stairs and then repeated the journey again and again. Love gives one the strength to bear any burden.

One month before Hurricane Katrina hit the United States, Mumbai was devastated by floods. Before that, the tsunami ravaged the coast of India and thousands died. At these times, hundreds of thousands of people were stranded and needed to be fed and clothed. People everywhere opened up their hearts to assist others who needed help. Food was cooked and served to those in need. No one ever went hungry in India. Every time there has been a disaster in India from floods to earthquakes, people have looked after each other.

In the Punjab area of Northern India, two trains crashed into each other in the early morning hours. The whole village awakened to help with the disaster. All the farmers started up their tractors and shined their headlights on the site of the accident to provide light for the rescue work. The survivors were shivering from the cold, so farmers sacrificed their precious haystacks to make huge bonfires to provide warmth for the people.

A hospital was created in a nearby temple. The village head chose a team of people to take care of the victims' money and valuables and kept a full inventory of their belongings. Not a single rupee was lost or stolen. The farming village had a population of only a few thousand people but still they were able to feed 50,000 people each day for over a week. Love and compassion for those in need was the spontaneous response that overcame all boundaries of caste and creed.

Even though we cannot all perform such heroic deeds, we can at least try to practice acts of simple loving kindness towards those around us. All actions can become ones of selfless love if they come from innocence and are offered genuinely without attachment or expectation.

One day a very old man went for Amma's darshan at the ashram. He must have been almost 90 years old. When he went up to Amma he said very seriously, "Amma, if you ever need any *influence* just let me know, because my father used to be a cook in a very high-up politician's house. So just let me know Amma, and I can try and help you out some time!"

Both this man's father and the politician must have died years before, as he himself was so old. But it was the only thing that he could offer to Amma, so he was gladly offering from a heart full of love.

Even if the gesture is small, we should all try to help others in whatever way we can. Our life is just like an echo – we get back precisely what we give. If we give love, then it will surely come back to us.

Chapter 8

Miracles of Faith

When you come to the end of all the light you know and it's time to step into the darkness of the unknown, faith is knowing that one of two things shall happen: Either you will be given something solid to stand on – or you will be taught to fly.
Edward Teller

Faith, like love, is intangible. The qualities of faith are indescribable, yet they are the very foundations of life. While we may have miraculous experiences that deepen our faith, our faith should not depend on these experiences.

God has no need for our faith; it is we who need God's grace.

Once Amma's brother-in-law went to his birthplace to see his mother, but his mother would not speak to him. He did not know why, so he went to visit a temple and prayed to the deity of *Devi* inside the sanctum of the temple saying, "I do not know why my mother is not speaking to me. I feel very sad."

At that time, his wife was visiting the ashram and her son was playing with Amma. Amma told the little boy, "Oh your poor father, he is so sad. He is praying to Devi in the temple because his mother is not speaking to him. You tell him not to be sad."

Later that day when they were back at home, the little boy told his father what Amma had said. His father was taken aback as he had not told anyone about his prayer. He discussed the event with his wife, because at that time he did not have a lot of faith in Amma. His wife assured him with a smile that it was not such a big thing for Amma to know of his prayer to Devi in the temple. Slowly his various experiences with Amma, his Divine sister-in-law, brought him to the point where he could no longer doubt Her Divinity.

When Amma was a teenager and performed the first "miracles," She never wanted any recognition. When people claimed that She had done something great by performing a miracle, Amma said, "We cannot create that which is not already there."

Amma says the real miracle is transformation of mind. To attain peace of mind – *that* is the genuine miracle.

To strengthen our faith, Amma may satisfy our desires. Countless are the instances where people's wishes have been fulfilled, but Amma wants us to go beyond the state of senselessly craving. Her emphasis always lies in teaching us spiritual lessons.

A massage therapist living in Amritapuri had just recently given up her profession before meeting Amma. She felt too overwhelmed by the magnitude of everyone's pain, which she knew extended much deeper than the physical. She felt that until she had pure love to give, that she could not truly help anyone through massaging them. She knew that Amma was the only one who could instill in her the depth of untainted love that she had been searching for her whole life.

Upon first meeting Amma, she had immediately wanted to serve Her by massaging Her. One day at breakfast she heard two people talking about massaging Amma. She asked them if they thought it might ever be possible for her to do so. They shook their heads and said it was not possible. One woman jokingly said that she should try and ask anyway, but that Amma would probably say something like, "Yes, one day I'll call you." The woman felt sad, thinking that she was too impure to serve Amma in this way.

A week later there was a Christmas play held in the ashram auditorium. Amma was sitting on a chair, surrounded by ashram residents, watching the play. The young woman noticed that Amma was rubbing Her neck a little as if it was paining Her, and so she thought perhaps this was the perfect chance to massage Her. The massage therapist in her could not bear to see Amma in pain, knowing that she might be able to do something to relieve it.

She prayed to Amma to please let her be an offering and allow her to try to ease Her pain. She prayed for some sign indicating she should make the attempt to approach Her and massage Her. She requested inside, for Amma to turn Her head to the right, if She wanted her to come.

Amma immediately turned Her head to the right. Feeling a ripple of excitement, once again she prayed, *Oh Amma, I'm sorry, but I don't know if that was simply a coincidence. I really want to come and offer my only skill to you, but I'm not sure if I should make such a fool of myself as to come through this big crowd, so please give me another sign. Please just turn your head to the right again.* Amma instantaneously turned Her head to the right once again.

The woman became extremely nervous now and could not believe that this was actually happening. She started to doubt herself now and feared the public humiliation if she was wrong. She thought, *Why hadn't I thought of a more obvious sign, one more out of the ordinary? OK, I will come Amma, but I need just one more clearer sign. Please, please raise your right arm.* Without missing a beat, Amma dramatically raised Her right arm, really high in the air, to adjust Her sleeve.

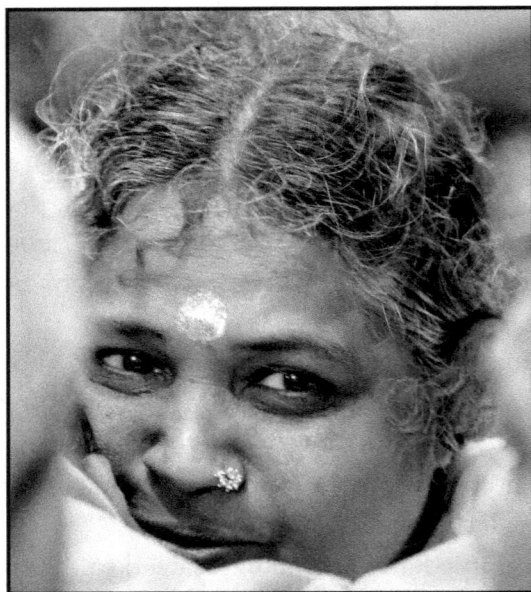

There was no doubt in her mind at all now – she just had to go up to Amma. Despite her fear, she got up and wove her way through the crowd. Everyone looked at her strangely, wondering why she was going up to Amma. When she got up to Her, she was extremely nervous. Amma looked a little taken aback by her sudden presence. She felt so silly, but still smiled and asked, "Amma do you want me to massage your shoulders?" Amma started speaking loudly in *Malayalam*. She decided that Amma was probably telling her, "No way!" so she turned and started to leave.

With a huge smile, Amma grabbed her chin, pulled her close and kissed her on the cheek. The young woman took this as meaning, "But, thanks anyway."

As she turned to make her way back through the crowd, all the *brahmacharinis* sitting near Amma said enthusiastically, "She said yes! She said yes!" They prodded her to go and stand behind Amma's chair and start massaging Her.

She stood behind Amma, but her usually competent hands stopped dead in their tracks above Amma's shoulders. She inwardly prayed, *Oh my goodness, the Goddess of the Universe is letting me massage Her. How can this be? I don't know how to proceed. Oh great Goddess, how do you want me to massage you?* At that moment Amma turned around laughing and said, "Press!" So she began to press down on Amma's shoulders. She stayed there the duration of the whole play and massaged Amma to her heart's content.

Later when someone came to talk to Amma, her attention was diverted. In that moment, Amma abruptly turned around and told her to take her seat again. She sat down nearby, feeling a little sad at having lost her concentration, but pleased to have had her desire fulfilled. She realized it was a precious teaching for her that we should stay focused on the goal.

No one could believe that Amma had let this newcomer massage Her, especially for so long. But she knew Amma had compassionately answered her prayers with this rare blessing to help her to continue serving others without letting her talent go to waste.

Some weeks later, Amma told her the only way to become pure is through service, and that even though her intentions may not be fully selfless yet, that she should just keep serving and the ego will gradually diminish. This young woman now offers massage again and has dedicated her life in the quest to become an instrument of pure love by serving others.

Our faith increases when we realize that Amma truly does hear our hearts' desires.

A young woman in Australia was a little afraid before her operation to remove a wisdom tooth. Her mother tried to comfort her by insisting that Amma would be with her all through the operation. Her mother said that she should visualize Amma as the Divine doctor performing the surgery. Liking this idea the girl sang to herself *My Sweet Lord* as she received the anesthesia. She still had the words in her mind as she faded into unconsciousness, quietly thinking about Amma.

When she woke up after the operation, she heard the melody of *My Sweet Lord*. It was a real shock to her. At first she thought she must be dreaming but she realized she was awake. After looking around in surprise she then thought she must be hallucinating. She inquired with the staff and discovered the source of the song – it was playing on the radio. With great delight she realized that Amma really must have been with her all along and was looking after her.

A devotee's sister was in the Intensive Care unit in the hospital after an operation. A little girl visited her every day. The little girl was very sweet and her presence filled the woman with a joy that gave her the energy to recuperate quickly. This young girl caressed her forehead and pulled the sheet over her when she needed it. The woman assumed the little girl was a daughter of one of the nurses or other patients. She asked the girl her name and where she came from, but the little girl would not reply. She visited every day for a few days, until the woman was transferred out of the I.C. unit.

As she was leaving the hospital, the woman told her brother and the nurses about this wonderful child who had helped her recover. The nurses replied that children are not allowed in the I.C. and it was not at all possible for there to have been a child there. They concluded that the woman must have been hallucinating. The woman's brother came to Amma during the darshan time and related this story. Amma turned to the others on the stage and innocently, with a look of wonder on Her face asked, "Who could that little girl have been?"

A man from Kodungallur told a story of his first experience of meeting Amma. He had been diagnosed with hepatitis that he had contracted years before from a blood transfusion. He had tried various treatments but nothing had worked, and so he decided to seek help from Amma.

When he went up for darshan he asked Amma if She could help him. She told him to get some Krishna *Tulasi* and bring it to Her. When he brought the tulasi up to Amma, She squeezed it with Her hands and created a juice from it. He drank the juice and was quickly cured of the hepatitis.

The faith that Amma inspires in us can help us to overcome what may otherwise seem to be insurmountable obstacles.

There was a lady who started out on her way to attend Amma's evening program but decided to stop along the way for a drink. One thing led to another and she ended up quite inebriated. Feeling that she had really missed an opportunity to be with Amma, she traveled to the program site. When she arrived, she discovered the doors of the building were locked and the program had finished a long time before.

Not quite in her normal thinking capacity, she decided to break into the building. Once inside, she went up to the front of the room and sat on Amma's peetham and cried and cried with sorrow and regret for being so stupid that she had wasted her time drinking. She felt that she was just a loser. She ended up lying down on the floor weeping in the same spot where Amma's feet had been.

The next day, she came to the program site again for Amma's darshan and remorsefully confessed to Amma what she had done the night before. Amma was extremely gentle and accepting with her. Amma's sympathy overwhelmed her and she decided that she could not let Amma down anymore. She had seen Amma several times and had told Her of the drinking problem, but Amma always comforted her with compassion and deep love, never chastising her. By Amma's grace the woman stopped drinking from that day on.

There was a family that visited the ashram in India every year for a holiday. Their son, who was about eight years old, had a bed wetting problem that profoundly embarrassed him. It was troublesome for his parents who constantly had to change his bedding and he was often teased about it. One year when the little boy came to visit Amma at the ashram, he was so upset about this problem that he insisted on seeing Amma in Her room. He shooed away Amma's personal attendant so he could confide in Her privately about his problem. As soon as he was alone with Amma, he took Her hand and started to guide it to his private parts, asking for Her to please bless him not to wet the bed anymore. Amma jumped in shock and called out to the others in the room to quickly come over. She laughed and laughed, relating the incident to the others, remarking on the little boy's absolute innocence and faith.

The next day at darshan Amma told the story to everyone. The young boy did not mind, because from that day onwards he was fully cured from his bedwetting and was never troubled by it again. We still remember this incident with the young boy who is now a few years older and is able to laugh along with everyone else.

When we approach the Guru with innocence, sincerity and openness, we will get some directions that shall guide us on the right path, even if we make a mistake along the way. This attitude of innocence also helps us to attain an element of deep peace and satisfaction in our lives.

People usually come to the Guru with many preconceived notions. It is difficult not to have certain expectations because we tend to judge the Guru intellectually. But the Guru's realm of existence is way beyond anything we can really understand with the intellect. Faith, accompanied by surrender and child-like openness, will enable us to attain a deeper understanding.

Abraham Lincoln is an example of someone who had immense faith and perseverance. He lost his elections regularly but still he did not lose heart. He contended in the elections again and again and finally became the president of the United States. Due to his determination, faith and hard work, the entire nation was benefited by his service. Though he was a consistent loser, he became a tremendous success. For him, failure presented just another hidden opportunity to progress.

Some people lose their devotion when they meet with difficulties. That kind of faith is not for the sake of devotion but is based on some kind of expectation. True faith needs to be steadfast and unwavering. Only with this kind of faith can we grow spiritually.

There was a villager who lived near Amma's ashram in India. He had a small business that prospered from the influx of people coming to the ashram. He was very grateful to Amma for this sudden success and felt devoted to Her because of it. Then, he unexpectedly experienced some trouble and as a result lost both the business and his family. Because of this tragedy, he also lost his devotion.

When we have strong faith, it cannot be shaken. Our faith helps us to face hard times as well as times when all is going smoothly. If our faith can be shaken, then it was not real faith after all.

Amma often insists that we put forth effort and then grace will surely come. This was certainly the experience for a young South American girl. At nine years old she was diagnosed with a congenital eye disease. The doctors had told her that she could completely lose her eyesight by the time she was 18 and she often worried about what would become of her life if she were blind. When she was 15 years of age she met Amma for the first time and confided in Her about this eye problem. Amma told her not to worry about it anymore, that She would definitely look after her.

When the girl finished school she was not sure of what she wanted to do and sought Amma's guidance on which career to embark upon. Amma suggested that she should try medicine. This completely astounded her as she had never thought herself smart enough to pursue that kind of career. Throughout her life she had only used naturopathic remedies, so the whole idea was quite overwhelming for her. But Amma insisted that she should simply try, so with full faith she enrolled at the AIMS medical college in India.

At times, she experienced severe obstacles, especially with the amount of studying that was expected of her and because of her weak eyesight. She also found it difficult because she had only learnt English a few years before, and so was not able to communicate properly with her professors or the other students.

There were occasions when the teachers chastised her in front of her classmates, insisting that it was crazy for her to be trying to pursue such difficult studies. Even for the brilliant young people that could understand the local language quite clearly, it was really tough. The teachers asked her how she could dare to presume that she could keep up with the rest of the students, considering all of her challenges. They insisted that she should go into nursing or dentistry, something simpler instead.

Feeling extremely dejected, she went to Amma to beg for permission to leave medical school. But Amma looked at her and said, "Amma wants you to stay, you have to try. When Amma told you to come to study, Amma had a purpose in mind, so you should stay. If you really try, you will be able to succeed."

This happened a few years ago. Amma's simple words of encouragement gave her the strength to hold on through all the difficulties. As a result of her passing with good grades, even her professors developed faith in Amma.

Sometimes when a Mahatma tells us something, we may not quite understand the exact meaning of the words. But if we have an open heart and mind, the correct understanding will eventually be revealed to us.

One of the ashram residents informed the others that he was supposed to take a trip overseas to his birthplace. He went to Amma to tell Her that he was going. Amma said, "No, you're not going now." He had someone to help him with the translation and together they tried to explain to Amma that he wasn't asking if he should go, but was simply informing Amma that he was going. Amma again said, "No, you're not going." The man was astounded. Not wanting to argue with Amma, he left feeling very confused. A little later he found out that he could not get a flight on his intended departure date, and there were other problems with the ticket that he did not know about – but Amma in Her own Divine way knew everything.

When we visited the city of Indore during the North Indian tour of 2006, there were a lot of surprises in store for us. Massive crowds of people refused to be controlled, but in the midst of chaos there were so many wonderful stories of people whose lives had changed dramatically. For instance, I heard the story of a woman who had been in a coma for three months. She was brought on a stretcher for Amma's darshan during the evening. Two days after receiving Amma's darshan she came out of her coma and returned to normal.

The woman who had helped bring all the disabled patients for Amma's darshan told me her own story. A single mother, she had raised three children on her own. When her children first heard about Amma one month before the program, they started to fall in love with Her. For the entire month the children had not wanted to listen to any radio or cinema music as they usually had. From morning till night they only played Amma's Hindi bhajans over and over again.

Wanting to help out with pre-tour work, her children walked miles and miles around the city sticking up posters announcing Amma's arrival and handing out pamphlets with information about the upcoming program. They had gone to institutions for the disabled to invite people for the program. The girl who was 14 years old and her ten-year-old brother arranged for meetings at their house to help coordinate transporting people to the program. Everyone excitedly looked forward to Amma's visit.

On the evening of the program her young daughter dressed herself in a colored sari and wore a crown. She also held the flag of India. She was portraying Bharat Mata (Mother India) and preceded Amma to welcome Her on the short walk up to the stage. However, because of the frantic pushing of the excited crowd, the girl became extremely frightened as we made our way to the stage and finally sat down. Utter chaos ensued as the stage filled up with aggressive and uncontrollable people who would not move from this area. But even worse was the area around the stage where a mass of excited people were all crammed together.

Bharat Mata stood on the floor just in front of the stage in a catatonic state. Amma grabbed her and quickly brought her on to the stage. Even though it was totally packed, the people made space for the frightened girl to sit near us. She was still in a state of shock and tears gently began to roll down her face.

As the evening progressed, the crowd went from absolute and utter chaos to slightly controlled chaos. Bharat Mata stayed on the stage the whole evening. Later on when I had the chance to talk with her, she said she was so happy to be here with Amma and even though she had been frightened by the crowd, she had yearned to have Amma's darshan and for the chance to sit near Her for a long time. That was exactly what she had prayed for and all her wishes had come true.

If we have innocent desires, God will surely fulfill them one day. A visitor from North India came to stay at the ashram for a few days. There was no public darshan scheduled for the day he arrived, so he decided to spend the day helping out working in the kitchen. He had a strong longing to have Amma's darshan and sincerely prayed for some miracle that he might be able to. He decided to fast for the day until he could see Amma. After working for long hours, he took a shower and changed his clothes and then returned to wait near the kitchen in case they needed more help.

All of a sudden, a few people brought over some chairs to be taken upstairs to Amma's house for a meeting with important guests and someone from the press. The man offered to carry the chairs. After he reached the top of the stairs and put the chairs inside the room, the door quickly shut behind him and he found himself enclosed in the room with only a few people and Amma. He was amazed but extremely happy and sat down quietly in the corner.

Amma spoke with several of the guests and then the reporter from the press had some questions for Her. One of the questions concerned the performance of miracles. Amma talked with the guests for quite a long time and then gave them darshan before they departed. Only one man was left in the room. Amma called him over and asked where he was from. He said that he was from Pune and admitted that he had been working in the kitchen all day. He had simply carried the chairs upstairs and then the doors had closed behind him, leaving him in the room. He confessed that he had a deep desire to have darshan with Amma, even though he knew it was not a darshan day. Amma had definitely answered his prayers.

We had to laugh – here was a miracle that the reporter had just missed. We had thought this man was one of the important guests. In all honesty, he ended up being the most important guest of the day as he had been working so hard in the kitchen. With his hard work, faith and innocent desire, he had earned his darshan and an apple from Amma to break his fast.

An Australian woman told me of her burning desire to be able to worship Amma's feet. She did not want to trouble Amma by asking for this – but still she could not forget her yearning. When Amma was in Australia later that year, She went down to the ocean side with a group of people. This woman found that she was standing next to Amma in ankle-deep water. It was a rare occasion to be with Amma with so very few people around. Realizing that Mother Nature was providing the answer to her prayers, this woman knelt down and with a heart full of devotion, gently poured a few handfuls of the seawater over Amma's feet. At last her prayers had been answered and the desire that she had held onto for such a long time had been fulfilled.

Amma answers all the prayers of an innocent heart – even Her own! During Amma's annual visit to Calicut, the nights are very long. On one of these nights, Amma finished the darshan program and returned to Her room in the early morning hours. She had not been eating very much over the previous days, so Her attendant thought that she would save a small treat for Amma to eat, an *unniappam*. After the one unniappam was eaten, Amma said that She wanted another one. Her attendant stated emphatically that there were no more, as she had been careful to put aside only one. Becoming quite child-like, Amma insisted that the attendant was not telling the truth, because She *knew* that there were more. The attendant insisted that she *was* telling the truth – there really were not any more at all. Amma again insisting that this was not true, came out of the room into the adjoining kitchen area to search for another one.

I was staying in a corner of the kitchen area and witnessed the silhouette of Amma as She entered the kitchen. I could just barely make Her out in the shadows, as the light was not on and it was quite dark. The attendant was following Amma and still declaring, "Honestly Amma, there are not any more."

Amma entered the kitchen and went straight over to the table and reached out in the dark. She found an unniappam that was sitting amongst lots of utensils and a large number of other things on the table. She went straight to it in the dark saying, "There you are!"

Amma walked away happily. Her attendant and I were both in awe that Amma had discovered what She was looking for in the dark and amongst the myriad of things on the table. The attendant had to eat her words, while Amma got to eat the second unniuppam. It was another display of Amma's miraculous powers in just one more simple down-to-earth way.

Chapter 9

Torrential Grace

Sometimes I go about pitying myself—
and all the while I am being carried
across the sky by beautiful clouds.
Native American saying

Amma has said that human beings can grow; they can grow and become God. We have the capacity in this life to achieve the Ultimate. However, one should also remember that within a moment's time everything can be lost. Just like a shadow, death is always walking behind us. Like an uninvited guest, death can tiptoe in and take everything away. This is why Amma says we should prepare ourselves to receive death at any moment and welcome it smilingly.

On a crowded darshan day in India a young girl's grandmother, using a walking stick, went up to Amma for darshan. She told Amma that she wanted to leave the body.

Amma replied, "Wouldn't your family miss you?"

"No. Amma should please let me go." Amma reluctantly agreed, and 15 minutes later after darshan, the old woman fell down near the elevator and died. Although death is usually considered a sad event, everyone felt extremely happy for her, because she had received Amma's blessings and had the grace to go so quickly and painlessly. Her heartfelt wish had been fulfilled.

Amma will let some leave and She may make others stay. A new resident of the Amritapuri ashram had been a nurse in the United States. On her first trip to Amma's ashram in India, she traveled with the tour to Calicut in northern Kerala, for a very intense few days of programs. This woman was delighted to be on tour with Amma for the first time. She had always dreamed of what it would be like to travel with Amma in India.

During one program Amma called all the Westerners to sit on the stage. Because of rheumatoid arthritis, this woman needed to sit on a chair. She did not want to block anyone's view of Amma, so she sat near the edge of the stage. After about an hour of quietly focusing on Amma, out of the blue, she felt her chair falling backwards and then upside down. While falling off the stage, she had the powerful intuition that her body was going to die. She fell directly on her head. There was a flash of bright light and then everything went dark.

The next thing she could remember was the tour doctors hovering over her asking questions, but she could not form any words to answer. While examining her, one of the doctors discovered signs of severe brain swelling. Another doctor reported that she had no reflexes and that her body was limp. She could not feel her body at all and the only sense that was intact was her hearing, for she could hear everything going on around her. In her heart she was calling out for Amma. All she remembers thinking was, *Amma I just got here, please let me be with you, don't let me go now.* People reported that the only words coming out of her mouth over and over again were, "Amma, Amma, Amma."

Abruptly, she felt herself leave her body and float upwards, but she could see that she was still attached to the body by a cord. She was hovering above, listening to the screaming of the people down below, but she could barely hear them. She felt miles away and knew she was dying.

She was put on a stretcher and brought to Amma. Amma bent down really low so the woman could see Her face. Amma put Her hands on the woman's chest and asked her how she was feeling. She felt the back of the devotee's head. All the while Amma looked greatly concerned. She put Her hand on the woman's forehead and her eyes automatically closed. The woman felt she was in a profoundly peaceful place full of golden light, for what seemed like a remarkably long time. Then Amma removed Her hand. The woman's eyes opened and she was back in her body. Amma began kissing her face and hands. After a few kisses Amma asked, "Okay? More?" and began kissing her again.

She felt that Amma was like a doctor assessing Her patient's well being and helping her to be able to interact with the world again. Amma then said, "Scan, scan, hurry, hurry!" and she was taken away to the hospital. The CAT-scan showed severe swelling between the skull and the scalp as well as bleeding from the skull. The doctors told her that it was a miracle, because such severe swelling outside the brain is almost always associated with a lethal brain injury.

While in the emergency room, she slowly began to function normally again, and was able to talk and move her hands. She was sent back to the Amritapuri ashram and told to lie flat on her back for three weeks. Periodically she would go to Amma for darshan and Amma conducted Her own style of medical examination, insisting that she rest and wear a surgical collar when not resting. After the third week, Amma asked her if she had pain anywhere. In that moment, she realized that her chronic arthritis pain had completely vanished. Amma smiled teasingly and said, "Maybe collar off in a few days, we will see." Amma let her remove the collar one week later. Doctors felt that her recovery was an act of grace, and the woman *knows* that it was Amma's grace alone that kept her alive.

There are endless stories of Amma's timely interventions protecting Her children from greater harm. A Sri Lankan devotee helping during the Australian tour of 2006, was invited to make some flower garlands for Amma for the program in Perth. She worked hard for three days, sometimes forgoing sleep. As a reward for her hard work she was invited to garland Amma at the airport as Amma was departing for Her next stop on the tour. The woman accepted the offer happily. At the airport she garlanded Amma. To the woman's surprise Amma removed the garland after a little while and gave it back to her, which was unusual. Immediately after this happened, Amma grabbed this woman's daughter from the group of children waiting for Her and started walking with both the mother and daughter. Then along the way, She took hold of the child's grandmother out of the crowd and walked with all three of them. A little further along she paused and took hold of the woman's husband and then gave all four of them a loving embrace. Everyone was surprised that Amma picked the family members from the different places and brought them all together, even though they had not previously gone for Amma's darshan together.

A few months later, the woman's husband met with an accident while working at a mining site. Buried alive in a trench for at least seven minutes, he was unconscious when they pulled him out and took him by ambulance to the hospital. Nearly all of his ribs and also his shoulder blades were broken, so he was placed in an induced coma for several weeks. The doctors were not sure whether he would survive. Even if he did survive, they worried he might be permanently disabled.

The whole city hosted special prayers for his recovery. To everybody's surprise, he came out of danger very quickly. His progress was a mystery to the physicians. Only months later did the family realize why Amma had chosen them for a unique and special blessing together.

When the man had fully recovered, the local newspaper expressed interest in his story. He told them that he believed he was saved by Amma's sankalpa. He felt She had known about his accident even before it had occurred. He came to understand that their darshan together had actually been a lifesaving blessing from Amma. He and his family are eternally grateful to Amma for giving his life back and reuniting them.

A European woman staying in the ashram for a long time confided in me that she was always worried about not having the money to live with Amma in India. She did not want to go back to her country to work to make money; she only wanted to stay in the ashram to perform service for Amma. She did not tell anyone else about this, but secretly prayed to God to find some solution for her. She wondered if God would hear her prayers.

Amma of Her own accord called her one day and told that she should stay in the ashram even though she did not have any money. Because of her surrendered attitude, her silent prayers were answered.

A devotee in Bangalore was recovering from a major operation. Because of this, she was totally unable to sit on the floor. During Amma's visit to Bangalore, she attended the program and late in the evening she decided to go to the dining room for her dinner. She had previously seen that there was only one chair in the whole dining room, so she was concerned that it would be difficult for her to eat standing up. She entered the dining room and was very surprised to find the single chair was not being used, even though the area was full of people. The devotee felt Amma was with her, guiding and protecting her even in this small gesture, holding her hand along the way to recovery.

When we put forward sincere effort with an innocent heart, a flow of grace will surely come to us. One of the young students living in the ashram told me that she had completed two assignments for her college course while she was on tour, working as full-time staff at the bookstore. She had studied in her spare time under the craziest conditions – in a closet, under the table – and always with so many distractions. Later, she was shocked to find out that for these two assignments she had received her highest grades ever. We felt that this was tangible evidence that the flow of grace simply comes to us from the effort we put forth.

One of the brahmacharinis who teaches at the Amrita University, said that if she ever feels that she knows something about the subject that she is about to teach, the class never goes well. However, when she realizes that she really does not know anything at all, then Amma's grace kicks in to fill in all the gaps, and she is successful in teaching the class.

The attitude of "I" and "mine" is the greatest obstacle to obtaining God's grace. When we are able to drop our attitude of self-importance, then wonderful miracles can happen. Amma is the greatest example of what happens when one becomes

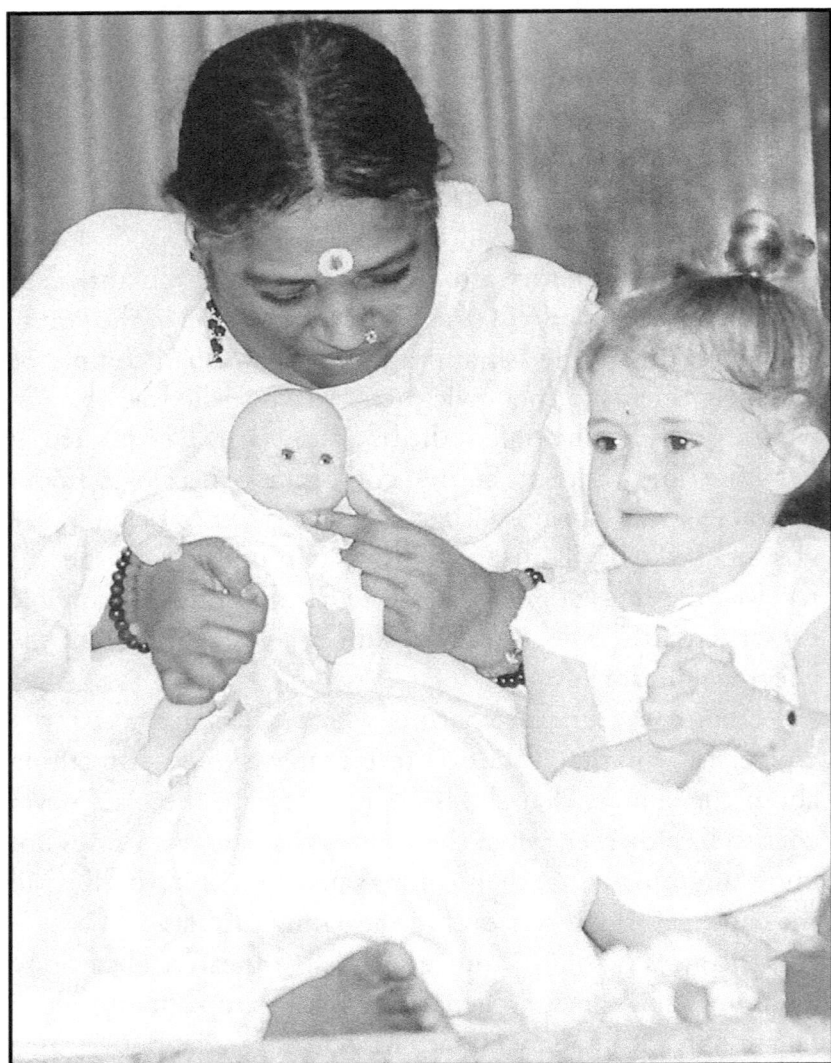

truly selfless. Her every action is imbued with divinity. She is an embodiment of love and compassion.

There was a little boy who used to come home from kindergarten everyday with a flower that he would place on the altar in front of Amma's picture. One day he brought a really dirty flower, and his mother told him not to put it on the altar. He said that Amma would still like it anyway, whether it was dirty or not. His mother could not really reply to this, so she just kept quiet.

Later that year, Amma was making Her annual visit to Mumbai, and the young boy was getting ready to go and see Her. He told his mother that Amma was going to give him back all the flowers that he had offered to Her. "Is that why you put them?" his mother asked.

The boy defended himself by answering, "No!" When they went to see Amma for darshan, he stood in front of Her with his hand held out. Amma took a large handful of flowers and showered them on his head. Still he had his hand held out open to Amma, so She took some more flowers and pressed them into his hand and closed his hand over them so they would not fall out. Then She said to him, "There! Is the account closed now?" He looked across and smiled to his mother as if to say, "See, I told you so!"

Amma says that She feels affection equally for everyone, but sometimes people's innocent love and devotion attracts Her thoughts towards them. When Her mind is simply drawn towards someone, when the remembrance of them comes to Her again and again, Amma feels this to be grace.

A situation happened where I really saw Amma in this state where I felt that surely Her grace was flowing. It was after a three-day program in Trivandrum. Amma had hardly any rest during this time – some days She had only an hour break between the morning and evening programs.

After the last evening program, there were four house calls scheduled. It was already mid-morning, and with no sleep we started out for the house visits. Just before the last visit Amma mentioned how extremely tired She was, but nothing could be done as She had promised to visit one more house.

On the way to the last house, we saw an elderly man who was waiting with a few other devotees by the side of the road. They were to drive the lead car to guide us to his home. Amma's face brightened when She saw that it was someone who had been devoted to Her for many, many years. Upon our arrival the men raced off to get into their car. A few seconds later they jumped out of the car and started pushing it along the road in order to try to jump-start the battery. We laughed at the funny sight, the beginning of our most memorable house call visit.

We finally reached our destination and were overwhelmed by the huge amount of people waiting for Amma's arrival. It was a very poor neighborhood but full of people who were deeply devoted to Amma. We made our way through the crowd, down the long pathway where the ground was covered in white cloth to protect Amma's bare feet. Eventually we reached a very small wooden house.

The crowd was filled with devotion and everyone clamored to be near Amma. It took a while to make our way through everyone into the small *puja* room in the center of the house. The devotee and his wife performed a *pada puja* and placed a pair of thin gold anklets around Amma's feet. They were incredibly happy – as this had been their dream for years. After performing the puja, Amma asked the man how his health was.

Like a small child he answered Her, "Oh Amma, I have not been able to sleep for ten days just knowing that You were coming!"

Amma usually takes the family into a separate room to talk privately for a few minutes. Looking around, She saw that they did not have any more rooms, as it was little more than a simple hut. Amma told the couple that they had to get some sleep now, after She left, as She knew that the wife was diabetic and the husband had previously undergone a triple bypass heart operation. Amma sensed that they had been up all night and was worried about them.

The crowd that had gathered waited eagerly for Amma's prasad. Instead of just handing something to each person, Amma decided to give each of them darshan. This seemed quite alarming to me, realizing that there were more than 100 people and knowing that Amma was so tired. But She wanted to bless each one of them. We found ourselves being pushed in one way or another by the desperate people waiting for Amma's darshan.

I sought refuge near the small puja room at the edge of the crowd. Inside, one of the local women was so overcome with devotion that she was tearfully praying and telling all of her problems to God. She seemed desperately sad and extremely devoted. Our photographer was profoundly moved and spontaneously started to give her own "darshan" to this woman. I was surprised to turn around and see her embracing the woman tightly and wiping away her tears. Amma was at one side of the room quickly giving darshan to everyone, and our photographer was ten feet away in the tiny puja room giving her own consoling, warm embraces to this woman. Just being in the vicinity of Amma's overwhelming love can cause our hearts to overflow with compassion.

At the end of the darshan we made our way through the excited crowd to the car. As we drove off, I thought at first that Amma might have been totally pushed to Her limit with exhaustion, but instead, She was ecstatic. She smiled blissfully and all signs of fatigue had left Her.

She said, "That was wonderful. I am so happy that I had the chance to go to such a poor home. They must have very little, but they gave me these gold anklets. I really should give them back, but instead we can give them some money."

She told the brahmachari who was driving to make sure that all their medical needs were taken care of, and to find out if they needed anything and to acquire it for them. I could see that Amma's heart was overflowing with love and concern for this elderly couple. Even when we had driven a long way, Amma continued to think about them, and again told the brahmachari not to forget about helping them. She said, "Oh I hope that they get some sleep now, as I know they did not sleep and I am afraid for their health if they don't."

Even though She had hardly slept more than a few hours in the past few days, Amma was worrying about the sleep and health of Her children. I could really see how Amma's mind and heart were drawn towards these people because of their innocent devotion. I could feel Amma's grace flowing towards them.

We often think that only people who deserve something should be given it. But with Amma's all encompassing love, She feels that especially those who may not deserve something should have the chance. Otherwise, how can they learn to change?

While entering the United States one year, we were going through the immigration formalities, and the man working at the desk asked Amma if She had Her husband traveling with Her. I answered on Her behalf and translated to Her what he was saying. I was laughing to myself at the thought of Amma being married. Amma also had a surprised look on Her face when I repeated in Malayalam what the man had asked Her.

Amma continued to look surprised and so I repeated what I had said several times, and then finally said it again in English. Amma kept quiet. Later on, after we had left the airport and were traveling in a van, Amma laughed as She related how I had translated for Her. She told everyone that I had said, in Malayalam, that the immigration man asked if She had any cockroaches with Her. She thought that perhaps they suspected that some had climbed into our luggage in India and were checking on this since they are extremely strict nowadays.

Amma jokingly says that She has even lost the use of Her own language since She spends so much time listening to those of us who do not speak it correctly. No matter how many mistakes we make She accepts us, and unceasingly showers Her torrential grace upon us. Amma could have smart, young, intelligent people serving Her. But for some unknown reason – an act of grace – Amma allows people like me to serve Her. Her compassion and patience are, in fact, even greater than Her love.

Chapter 10

Relentless Effort

*"What is the secret of your success?" someone
asked Dr. George Washington Carver.
He replied, "I pray as if everything depends upon
God, then work as if everything depends upon me."*

When Buddha lay on his deathbed, he noticed his young disciple Ananda was quietly weeping. "Why are you weeping Ananda?" he asked.

Ananda replied, "Because the light of the world is about to be extinguished and we will be in darkness."

The Buddha summoned up all his remaining energy and spoke what were to be his final words on earth: "Ananda, Ananda, be a light unto yourself."

Amma reminds us of the same thing again and again. She tells us, "In reality we all have an infinite capacity inside of us. Holding a small candle in our hand we may think, *How can I go forward in the darkness?* But we have to just keep on moving forward, step by step, and the darkness will gradually disappear."

Some people desire to reach the goal without much effort. They are always looking for some short cut without putting forth any effort. But as Amma says, as more and more discounts are given, quality also decreases. We have become lazy. Amma was making the point that Self-realization cannot be given. It has to come from a gradual blossoming of the heart due to relentless effort on the part of the seeker, which may culminate in the Guru's grace. It cannot be forced or demanded.

Amma is always one to put in maximum effort to serve as an example for us. In the early days, Amma was the first one to start any work that needed to be done in the ashram. She made the first bricks that were used to build the ashram, and was the first one to climb into the septic tank to clean it. When people started to join the ashram, Amma told them that they should never become like a parasite. Instead they should work hard and be self-sufficient – and Amma has always led the way in being the one to work the hardest. She has always taught by personal example, not by mere words.

Amma instructed the brahmacharis how to make hollow bricks using cement and sand. Each brahmachari was instructed to make ten bricks. Amma told them to remember how much cement and sand they had used, to assure that they had mixed it in the right proportion.

One brahmachari decided to write in the sand the amount of sand and gravel he had added, but after some time forgot to mark the amounts. Sometimes he added a little more cement. Then he would think, *Oh, the cement is more so I should add a little more sand.* Then he would add a little more sand and repeat the same process all over again. After a while he finally started to make the bricks. When he finished ten bricks, there was enough mixture remaining to make another ten bricks but he thought, *I have made my ten bricks. That is all I was told to do. Let the rest go anywhere,* and went back to his hut to rest.

When Amma found out there was rough material lying around going to waste, She called the brahmachari and said, "Why did you waste so much material?"

He answered, "Amma, I have done my duty. You asked me to make ten bricks, and you can see my ten bricks are ready. I don't know about the amount that is left behind."

Amma never ceases trying to teach the ashram residents how to work selflessly with alertness and awareness. This is not an easy task because our *egos* are so tenacious.

After a program had finished in Palakkad in 2006, we directly traveled to Trissur for the next program. While in the car, Amma kept mentioning that She would like to spend some time with the brahmacharis that had been working tirelessly at Nagapattinam, building the tsunami houses. Her mind was constantly thinking of them while we were traveling. All along the way, She was checking to make sure that their vehicle was close by. As soon as we arrived my first question was, "Where can I go to sleep?" Amma's first question was, "Where are the brahmacharis? Call them," as She wanted to sit with them.

Everywhere we go in the world, as soon as we arrive in a new city, Amma always sits and talks with the local people for a while, even after traveling all night. It does not matter how tired She may be or how late it is. In 2005 while traveling internationally, we had been in various airplanes for almost 48 hours when we finally arrived in Zurich for the start of the European tour. Upon arrival at our accommodation at a devotee's house, Amma never even made it to Her room. She sat down with the local devotees in the passageway outside Her room, and then proceeded to practice all Her new bhajans in German, as She knows how happy it makes people to hear Her sing in their mother tongue. Even though She may be physically tired like the rest of us, Amma has the power of mind to take Her above the physical limitations of the body.

One will find that although Amma has to sit for many hours in the same position, Her posture usually remains perfect. While we are on the stage and I have to sit for only a fraction of the time that Amma has to, I find myself often squirming around and fidgeting. Amma sits perfectly still in the same position, although just like me, She may also be experiencing leg pain.

Amritavarsham50 was an extremely hectic four-day event filled with numerous programs, but with very little food and sleep for us. At the end of the final program, Amma took a little rest and then traveled back to the ashram.

One of the swamis who did not usually travel with Amma had the rare chance to ride back to the ashram in the front seat of the car. Amma had been discussing the clean-up that would have to take place to assure that the stadium site was left completely clean. After we had gone a short distance, She unexpectedly stopped the car and asked the swami to go back and check to see that the toilets were properly cleaned and that everything was left in a better condition than we had found it. He was happy to sacrifice his chance to travel with Her, because he knew how important it was to Amma that an example be set, by leaving the stadium in good order.

Amma called another brahmachari to join us as we continued on our journey. As we traveled back to the ashram, I could barely stay awake. But Amma, who had given darshan to over 50,000 people in a 24-hour period, was wide awake. She sat forward on the edge of the back seat the whole way from Cochin to Amritapuri, discussing the events of the past few days with us. While She sat erect, Her back completely straight and never touching the back of the seat, I was slumped across the other side of the seat, exhausted. This is often the case. I am like a battery that runs out after some time, unlike Amma who is always connected directly to the Source!

On the 2006 North India tour, we had been in Mumbai for a few days of programs. After a large public program we went back to stay at the Nerul ashram on the outskirts of the city. Amma had not rested at all. She had not even gone to the bathroom the whole night. On arrival at the ashram She immediately went over to one side of the main hall and started to investigate the clutter that was stored there.

Amma has the habit of going directly to wherever things may be hidden, not wanting to be found. She will go exactly to that spot. She went over to a place where some unnecessary items were stored in the corners of the hall and started to straighten these items up. As space was very limited in the ashram hall, She was making room for people to sit for the upcoming programs. She worked Her way along all the sides of the hall, and right around the back of the ashram. Luckily there are always lots of willing workers that turn up when Amma starts to work. When She initiates the work, She knows it can be finished very quickly.

As She worked Her way around the building, cleaning and rearranging things, Amma found all the areas that had been overlooked. There was a pile of boxes of bookstall articles that She knew might be left there, taking up space, so She told us to move all these things so a few more people would be able to sit. Always thinking of others, Amma puts forth effort, even after a long night's darshan, to show us that the work is never done.

Wherever we go in the world, in addition to everything else She is doing, Amma is always the ever-vigilant building inspector. Nothing that anyone may wish to hide will ever escape Her gaze. Even though Amma had very limited formal education, Her knowledge and guidance extends into many different arenas.

When we visited Amma's ashram in Trissur last year, we arrived to a barrage of blinding flashes from the press photographers. I could not even see properly afterwards because the flashes had been so strong.

After this, I was really amazed when we walked on towards Amma's room, that She stopped just outside the room and pointed to the ground, saying "*Look!*" She was looking down at a small crack in the concrete floor. I do not know how She was able to see this, as I was still half-blind from the camera flashes. Amma said, "They did not pour the water properly when the concrete work was done." Amma entered Her room disappointed with the lack of care and attention on the part of the workers. Nothing can ever escape Amma because She is always alert in every situation, no matter where we are.

On the few occasions that we have visited the AIMS hospital, the doctors with us have proudly tried to show Amma the latest medical technology that they have acquired. Instead of admiring their equipment, Amma is usually examining the chips in the floor and the places where a ceiling tile may be missing, and pointing out where people have been careless.

She is constantly trying to teach us how to perform our actions properly, taking care not to misuse or waste anything.

Once in Santa Fe, an evening program finished very late. As usual, it was morning by the time the darshan had ended. We all went to bed even later, and everyone was exhausted – except for Amma. She took advantage of this quiet moment in the house to visit the kitchen and started to eat some ice-cream from the freezer. Her attendant stealthily followed Her, and was alarmed to see what Amma was eating for breakfast. She went straight to the room where I was staying and woke me up, exclaiming that Amma would not listen to her and that I should come and try to stop Amma from eating the ice-cream.

It was a daunting prospect to think of how I would be able to stop the Divine Mother of the Universe from eating ice-cream if She wanted to.

Lucky for me, by the time I got to the kitchen Amma had stopped eating the ice-cream. (She must have heard that I was on my way, and decided not to eat anymore out of fear of me.) By the time that I reached the kitchen, Amma was telling stories of the olden days to the few people that had gathered there.

Amma told a story of one time many years earlier when She had entered the old ashram kitchen to find one of the brahmacharis with his hands behind his back trying to look innocent, his foot on top of a sack of rice. Knowing his guilt, Amma proceeded to look behind the sacks stored in the small storeroom. To his horror, She immediately discovered a plate that he had just hidden. When She lifted the cover off of the plate, She found a large serving of rice with lots of rich *sambar* powder piled on top of it, and another sprinkling of rice on the very top to hide what was underneath. She reprimanded him for taking so much of the rich powder that was known not to be good for the practice of *brahmacharya*. In those days food was sometimes scarce, so we all found our own very ingenious ways to scavenge something out of nothing from the limited supplies available in the kitchen. Although we often try to hide things from Amma, She will always find out what we have done.

Years ago on the first retreat that Amma gave in Australia, we stayed in the rustic sea-side village of Somers, near

Melbourne. After the morning darshan Amma returned to the house where She was staying. She walked into the kitchen, went straight over to the compost bin and proceeded to plunge Her arm directly into it. She pulled out half a coconut. She said to the girl cooking that day, "What is this, daughter?"

The girl mumbled, "It's half a coconut, Amma." Amma inquired, "And what is it doing in the rubbish bin?"

The girl replied, "Oh it's got some mould on it." Amma picked up a spoon and scraped away the small piece of mould replying, "The rest of this can still be grated and used in the cooking. Don't waste food daughter."

In Her life, Amma has seen so much suffering due to poverty and the lack of basic necessities, which is why She is very strict with us when She finds that we have created unnecessary waste. Everyday, hundreds of people come to Her with heart-wrenching tales of hardship due to the lack of proper food, money or medicine. Because of this, Amma never misses an opportunity to attempt to teach us an important point through our everyday actions. She tries Her utmost to always guide us in the right direction.

Hundreds of people ask Her questions and write Her letters everyday. Amma tries to reply to all of them, but She has Her own way of answering. We may not always receive a direct answer, but we should have the faith that She has heard us. Sometimes She may not answer us because She says there are some things that we must learn directly from life itself.

In 2004, Amma had felt that something might interrupt the U.S. tour. It turned out that the Parliament of World Religions invited Amma to be a keynote speaker at a conference held in Barcelona, Spain, right in the middle of the tour. At first She was hesitant to go for the program, but in the end She

agreed to attend, to give Her European children the joy of being able to see Her more than once in a year. Devotees came from all over the world – from Finland, England, Germany, France, Denmark, and Switzerland. People attended from almost every country. They were all ecstatic to see Amma.

Amma had remarked that She would give a spontaneous darshan to people on the side of the hall after Her speech. She was not going to give prasad, but just a quick darshan to those that wanted one. In the end, Amma was invited to give darshan in a tent that had been prepared by a Sikh community that had come from London to serve free food to all the conference attendees. Amma gave a slow, loving darshan to everybody, to all the thousands of people who turned up. There were no formal darshan lines or tokens. The swamis and other musicians sang without a sound system in the dimly lit tent.

When Amma finished the darshan, She fed dinner to all of those remaining in the tent. Amma supervised the division and serving of the food. The original meal of an apple, three chapattis and curry, was cut down to one quarter of an apple, one chapatti and a little curry. Amma painstakingly took over an hour to feed 1,000 people with food that was intended for 150. Everyone was in bliss from having been so lovingly served, and could not believe that Amma could give so much of Herself.

At 3:00 a.m. we finally arrived back at the house where we were staying. We were on the verge of exhaustion, as we had traveled directly from the U.S. that morning and were due to return in a few hours. But Amma was still going strong. She did not want to sleep as the rest of us did, but wanted to discuss various points of the speeches.

No one can ever keep up with Amma. In fact, it takes several people working different shifts to keep up with Her. One of the swamis took Amma by the arm and escorted Her to the room that She was supposed to rest in, begging Her to try to get some sleep, as he lovingly closed the door with Her inside. Everyone else retired to the rooms arranged for them, so happy that at last they could rest as Amma was safely in Her room.

Very quickly we drifted off to sleep, but a little later I was awakened by the sound of Amma's laughter. She was standing in the doorway of our room laughing at seeing us girls sleeping in a row like sardines. No one else woke up as they were absolutely so tired. I thought I would give Amma some freedom, so didn't follow Her.

A few hours later, when we arose, we found out that Amma had never gone to sleep at all. We boarded a plane again after spending less than 36 hours in Barcelona, and flew back to continue the U.S. tour. Who constantly flies halfway around the world like this, just to make people happy? Only Amma.

She never tires of serving others. On public darshan days at the Amritapuri ashram, Amma often gives darshan from morning right up until evening. After these long darshans She must be so exhausted, but out of Her compassion She usually goes directly to the stage for bhajans, and in this way sets an example for us all. Amma never misses an opportunity to inspire Her children – such is the tireless love of a God-realized Being.

Our destiny is actually the effort that we have put forth in the past. To earn grace we must put in the effort now, even starting from childhood if we can.

An eight-year-old girl who was visiting the ashram in India was extremely enthusiastic about attending the early morning *archana*. She went almost every second day with her mother. Her mother never asked her to, but when she woke her up in the morning her daughter immediately stood up and took her archana book, ready to go. At first, her mother thought she would fall asleep soon after the names began, but to her astonishment she followed all the 1,000 names. Sometimes she lost her place and asked her mother which name they were on, so her mother had to be more alert than ever.

After the 1,000 names and the arati, they would go to the inner shrine of the temple to see the image of *Kali* there, admiring her beauty. After the first archana, her daughter told her that she could not pronounce all the difficult names. Her mother assured her that this is normal and that most adults cannot even chant them properly. Her daughter innocently replied that she responded to each name with her personal mantra. Her mother was touched by the extra effort that her daughter had made.

When we travel in the West, people often ask me why we work so hard. But when we see what Amma is doing, never resting and always searching for yet another way to serve others, how can we simply sit idle? How can we ever repay anything, even a fraction of what She has given to us?

When I was young and had finished school, I enrolled in a nursing course, although there was a three-year waiting list for this to commence. I worked for two years and in that short time, I came to understand the shallowness of worldly life. I did not think about work again for several years – but then I met Amma.

I knew what my path was when Amma always encouraged me to work hard. In working hard and serving others we can forget ourselves. When we forget about ourselves and spend all our time trying to solve someone else's problems, then everything is automatically taken care of for us.

An enlightened Master gives us something as priceless as the understanding of the meaning of life, without expecting anything back. I feel the only thing that we can offer in return, is to do a little work for a good cause. We have nothing else to offer. All we can do is strive to make some effort. Even just that little bit of effort, that attitude of just wanting to try to do what we can – will bring grace.

Someone once asked Amma, "What is grace, and how does it work?" Amma answered, "Life is grace. We need God's grace for doing anything. Without it, we cannot live in this world. A compassionate heart will always have grace."

Chapter 11

The Rhythm of Life

*Life is not about how fast you run, or how
high you climb - but how well you bounce.*

Anonymous

Amma says that everything in Nature has a rhythm – the wind, the rain, the ocean and also the growth of plants. Similarly, life itself has a rhythm – the flow of breath and even our own heartbeat. Our thoughts and actions create the rhythm and melody of our lives. When we lose the rhythm in our thoughts, it reflects in our actions. This in turn, throws off the very vibration of our life.

It is necessary to maintain the rhythm of the mind and body not just for the sake of health and individual life-span, but also for the sake of all humankind and Nature. The loss of this cadence is reflected in the natural environment and in society, through various disasters such as earthquakes and tsunamis. The balance of Nature depends upon humanity.

When we violate the laws of Nature we suffer painful con-sequences; but this pain serves as a reminder that something is wrong with our way of living. The longer we go on making the same mistakes, the more consequences we will accumulate and the more pain we will have to undergo. The actions we take in life will surely come back to us in one way or another, both the good deeds and the bad.

A news report related the following story. An armed robber entered a shop, made his way up to the cashier and put a $20 bill on the counter. As the cashier opened the cash register, the robber demanded, "Give me all the money that is in there – fast." The cashier saw the weapon in the man's hand, and quickly took all the money out of the cash register and gave it to the robber. The thief took it, hurriedly pushed it into his pocket and ran outside. In his haste, he made the mistake of forgetting to take back the $20 bill that he had placed on the table.

At the time of the robbery, there had not been much money in the register, only about $14. Instead of losing money, the shop gained $6 in the end. When we impose our selfish will and disturb the natural cycle of events by trying to take a short-cut, we usually end up short-changed in one way or another. We should instead be looking for opportunities to restore balance and harmony in our lives and in the world.

After the tsunami, a small puppy survived the killer waves. She was named Bhairavi because of her strength to survive. We could not keep her in the ashram, so a kind-hearted devotee took the puppy home with her. This devotee had been suffering from a chronic illness, and when she developed some red eczema-type sores on her feet she just presumed that they were a symptom of her illness. She visited many doctors, but none of them could explain exactly what they were, why she was suffering from them or offer any cure. She endured the skin problem for nearly 18 months.

Her little puppy used to chew on everything. One day Bhairavi chewed up her favorite pair of old, rubber sandals that she loved to wear. Immediately afterwards, the puppy started to develop red patches on her skin. But in the meantime, the red patches on the devotee's feet totally disappeared. She realized that the rash must have been caused by an allergy to the footwear. The mystery of her strange symptoms suddenly unraveled and she never again suffered from these problems. The puppy returned the favor to her for saving its life.

Human beings tend to think that they are so great. But Amma says that even the worms in excreta have families and love each other. What is the difference between them and us? The only difference is that humans are endowed with the ability to discriminate between what is right and wrong.

Once we try to refine this quality of discrimination more deeply, it naturally culminates in the virtue of compassion. We can then rise above all the lower tendencies buried deep within us that trap us like slaves. Then our lives gently begin to blossom, like the budding of an exquisite flower.

God's grace will truly flow from all directions to those who develop compassion and express it outwardly to suffering humanity. But if we do not use our discrimination, our lives will become stagnant, like a polluted pool of water. Then there is absolutely no difference between the animals and us, except animals may exhibit more selfless love than we do.

We were traveling in a vehicle one day when Amma explained to somebody, "Animals do not make any more *prarabdha* karma for themselves – unlike people who are always making more and more for themselves."

When animals are sick, they fast. No one can make them eat anything when their basic instinct is telling them to let the digestive system rest and dissolve the problem that has manifested. But this is not the case with human beings. Even when our body gives us the signs that we are sick and that we should slow down and fast, we may ignore this message and go on eating foods that are harmful for us, never letting the body rest so that it can repair itself.

Animals have a basic instinct that takes over and makes them do the right thing. They act according to an intuition that comes naturally to them. On the contrary, in human beings the mind becomes our master and makes us slaves. We often follow the desires of the body and whims of the mind. Ignoring common sense, we are completely unaware of and out of tune with our higher intuition. In this state, we are more likely to suffer accidents or illness. We need to hone our intuition and learn to attune ourselves on both the physical and mental levels.

Pain is not always an enemy; sometimes it can be a great friend and teacher. A European man was on tour with Amma in India when he fell on the sidewalk and badly broke his ankle. Although excruciatingly painful for him, he was aware right from that moment that the accident was somehow destined to happen. He tried to totally surrender to his fate and make the most of an unavoidable experience. He had to slow down with his life, as he could not rush around anymore. He was also forced to accept help from other people because he was unable to do many basic things for himself. He recognized that there are an incredible amount of things for him to be thankful for, things that he had previously taken for granted. This personal experience of a state of helplessness, helped him to cultivate more patience and compassion for others who might have difficulties in their own lives. His whole mode of thinking adjusted, and he witnessed the entire event as a blessing in disguise.

We often want to make changes in the outside world. We wish to change others without transforming ourselves at all. But Amma reminds us that if we really desire to make the world different, we should change ourselves first, and then automatically transformation will occur in the outside world. In fact, life will often force us to experience circumstances where we have absolutely no choice but to change. This is all for our own evolution, further advancing us towards the state of perfection.

As Henry Miller said, "The world is not to be put in order, the world is order incarnate. It is for us to put ourselves in unison with that order." For us to bring our body and mind back into a state of equilibrium with itself and with the rest of existence, we should try to learn to follow a basic dharma of how to behave in the world. If we surrender to the situations that come to us gracefully, with discrimination and humility, then life will not have to teach us so harshly.

The rare and extraordinary individuals that have achieved the state of God-realization, have come to a complete understanding and balance within themselves, and also with the vibrations inherent in all of life. They have attained this state through the unmitigated power of their divine intuition and complete surrender to a higher power.

Even though Amma did not perform so much formal *sadhana* in Her life, She reached the pinnacle of human existence by coming to understand who She really is. For a number of years Her passionate devotion was often misunderstood for craziness. She would accept food offerings only from the animals around Her, not from any human being. She could not bear to accept anything from anyone, for no one understood what She was going through; only Nature understood. The birds dropped fish for Her and cows offered milk to Her directly from their udders. Because She was able to tune into the rhythm of life, Mother Nature nurtured Her and took care of all Her needs.

At that time, two dogs always stayed close to Her. Amma would often be lost in Her own private world of ecstasy, lying in the sand or near the water. One dog remained with Amma, while the other one would go off in search of food for Her. They never left Her completely alone, but took turns being with Her and watching over Her. If any stranger came near, the dogs growled protectively. Their love for Her never wavered. When Amma retreated from the world of sorrow and pain through Her states of *samadhi,* they quietly waited for Her to re-emerge.

There was a time when Amma survived only on tulasi leaves for several months. Her experience proved that when the mind and soul become one with the divine internal vibration and rhythm of creation, the body can survive with little or no external sustenance.

Today, Amma eats and sleeps a little on most days because we insist that She should. She has so completely surrendered Herself to serve and comfort the world that She lets Herself come down from the highest realm of ecstasy. She brings Herself to our level of existence, sacrificing Her own state of bliss to try and inspire us to rise higher. Although She moves with us, dresses like us and may even sit and eat with us, Her mind totally dwells in another realm.

On one occasion, one of the women serving Amma filled a bucket of water and kept it ready for Amma to use for Her bath. This woman had not been careful filling the bucket and Amma noticed that there was some dirt floating in the water. Amma pointed it out, chastising her gently for not having noticed it.

The woman felt the freedom to ask Amma, "Why is it that sometimes Amma is not particular about cleanliness at all, and at other times Amma will notice the smallest speck of dust?"

Amma replied to her, "Sometimes I am in your world, and other times I am in Mine."

While traveling with Amma in India, we often sit by the side of the road in the late afternoon to meditate and then have a *chai* break. Along with the enjoyment of having a hot drink, Amma also conducts a question and answer session giving spiritual advice or simply asks someone to tell a story. On one of these occasions when we stopped by the roadside, everyone from the nine busloads of people traveling with Amma rushed to try and find a place to sit near Her.

After Amma sat down, one of the girls nearby attempted to pull out a small, prickly thistle plant that was growing very close to where Amma was sitting. When She saw this, Amma quickly stopped her from pulling out the plant. The girl remarked that it was only a weed, but Amma reminded her that everything has the same spark of consciousness flowing through it; therefore it would feel pain if she pulled it out and destroyed it.

Amma sees the essence of divinity in everything, and knows the pain that can be felt by even a leaf or a plant. For Her, the Supreme Consciousness is not just a concept, but something that is vibrating everywhere in everything. This knowledge of the Self unlocks all the secrets of Nature.

On the 2006 North Indian tour, we were traveling by road and stopped along the way. When we pulled over, Amma was given some special temple prasad that She wanted to distribute to everyone present. After giving some to each of us, She called the policemen who were escorting us and personally distributed the prasad to them as well. At that time, a dog turned up by

the side of the road. Amma insisted that the dog should be fed some as well. Someone started to place the food on the ground, but Amma wanted the dog to be fed from a dish. A blue plastic cover of a container was produced and Amma fed the dog with prasad on this. She wanted the dog to consume all of the prasad, so insisted that it lick every speck off the cover. After the dog had finished eating, Amma said the lid should be properly washed and returned, that it should not be thrown away. We all grimaced; horrified at the thought that the top of the plastic container would be used again, and it might end up that we would be eating out of it next. However, Amma had made Her lesson quite clear. Animals should be treated with as much respect as humans. One must see the same essence of divinity in all.

Amma knows that God is not just sitting up in the sky on a golden throne. The light of consciousness shines through every object and creature in this creation, both living and non-living. Unfortunately, we do not have the vision to see it.

Several years ago during the European Tour in Holland, Amma arrived at a devotee's house and went straight outside to pick an apple from a small, heavily-laden tree that She had seen in the garden. After She picked the apple, She begged forgiveness from the tree for taking fruit from it. She ate half the apple, then gave the rest as prasad to all the people that were there. She does not usually eat apples, but was drawn to this one particular tree. It must have been waiting for Her to offer itself.

Now every year when we travel to Holland, as soon as we arrive at the house, Amma goes directly outside into the garden. She takes only one apple from that same tree. This may be the one occasion for the whole year when She eats part of an apple. Amma said that when fruits are really ripe they taste delicious, but She feels incredibly sad to pick anything.

Sometimes, Nature has such a short lifespan that She feels it is better to let things live.

Mother Nature has innumerable spiritual lessons to teach us if we slow down enough to take notice. One evening we attended a public program where a massive crowd had gathered. In keeping with the tradition of Kerala, an elephant was at the site to honor the occasion. On this particular evening, Amma had alighted from the car and I was following Her through the crowd. We finally came to the elephant. Amma was delighted to see the elephant and went over to say hello to it. She turned to me and said, "Have you got anything to feed the elephant?"

The car was not close by, so I had to answer Amma truthfully that I didn't have anything to feed the elephant.

As you may know, Amma loves feeding elephants. But unfortunately, I was completely unprepared for this event. I don't usually carry a big bunch of bananas with me while we walk towards the stage for a program. Amma was shocked that I did not have any food with me to feed the elephant, and asked once again, "You don't have *anything* to feed the elephant?"

I had to laugh; silly me had forgotten to carry the elephant food with me. And you know how much elephants eat!

Amma was terribly disappointed and looked at the elephant with Her hands held up to show that She did not have anything to offer. As we walked off towards the stage, Amma kept turning around to the elephant to apologize for not having anything to give it, and was slightly gesturing towards me, as it was my fault that I had forgotten to carry the elephant food.

This was one good example showing that we must be prepared for all occasions in spiritual life. We never know what challenges life will bring us… and we never know when we will come across hungry elephants.

A young man from Malaysia related to me his experience of understanding the glory of Nature. He had purchased a small tulasi plant from Amma's program. Knowing that the plant was very sacred, he lovingly tried to nurture it for two weeks. He watered it at the same time every day, but after a few weeks noticed how dry and yellow it had become, with all of the leaves starting to wilt.

He remembered hearing from someone that the tulasi plant likes to listen to mantras, so he started singing a little and chanting some mantras to the plant, but its condition did not change. He innocently thought that maybe he had not sung loud or long enough, and worried that the precious plant was going to die. All of a sudden, he realized that he could probably play some bhajans to the plant by sitting it next to his computer and playing a CD of Amma singing. He soothingly spoke to the plant, telling it that this was the only other thing that he knew to do that might help it to recover. As he was tired from being at work all day, he went to sleep for about two hours while the music played. When he woke up and turned on the light, he saw that the plant was looking fresh and its leaves were not wilting anymore. He was absolutely astonished. Not believing his own eyes he rubbed them a little, in case his vision had been distorted from having just woken up. But the plant was looking revived, and the leaves had even become green again. He started to have a glimpse of understanding the magic of the power of sound.

Two weeks went by and he totally forgot about the incident. He normally kept the plant outside, remembering to water it at the same time every day. But once again it started to wilt, and the leaves began to turn yellow, although all the other plants near it seemed to be doing well. He decided to carry the plant inside once more, even though his parents thought he was quite crazy when he lovingly placed it next to his computer and turned the bhajan music on for it.

His mother had never really liked bhajan music so much, but he remarked to her that he would show her how special it really was, proving the revitalizing effect that it would have on the plant. She totally disbelieved that anything special would happen at all, and refuted the fact that there was something sacred about the vibration of the bhajans. Being Chinese, the Indian-style music was not at all to her liking, and she was constantly telling her son to turn the volume of the bhajans down.

He told her to look at the plant now, and then come back in one hour to see what effect the vibrations of the bhajans would have had on it. She returned in one hour and was taken aback to see that once again the plant had become refreshed, and the yellowing, wilting leaves had again turned green. This proved to her the purifying effect of the vibration of the bhajans, and she never again told her son to turn down the volume. The young man also comprehended something special from this experiment. Reflecting on the effect of the bhajans on the plant, he also started to contemplate the effect that Amma singing bhajans every night would surely have on all the people who heard Her, and even on the environment as well.

Life becomes complete only when humankind and Nature move in harmony, hand in hand. When melody and rhythm complement each other, music becomes beautiful and pleasing to the ear. Likewise, when people live in accordance with the laws of Nature, the song of life becomes sweet.

Chapter 12

Challenges On the Path

The biggest trouble-maker you will probably
ever have to deal with watches you shave
his face in the mirror every morning.

Anonymous

People often ask Amma how we should live in the world. Amma answers, "Live in the world like a flock of birds unattached to anything and ready to fly away at any moment."

When we were in Trissur in 2006 for a program, the weather was suffocatingly hot. Some of Amma's relatives came to visit but knowing how packed all the accommodations were they did not want to trouble anyone for a room. They just asked for two mats for the family to sleep on and happily slept outside on the ground. The wife said that since her husband never wanted to trouble anyone for anything, she was happy to sleep outside as well. She felt she was getting the chance to imagine what it was like at the ashram in the olden days when we sometimes used to sleep outside.

If we have a positive attitude about accepting all of life's situations no matter what they may be, then we can come to see God's hand in everything. We have been given this human birth in order to face challenges and overcome them – not to

135

run away from them. With God's grace we are always given the strength to be able to face everything that comes to us.

Amma reminds us that life may not always bring us good experiences. In fact, it may be that we have more bad experiences in store for us than good. Good and bad experiences are the nature of the world. However, we should learn to convert such challenging experiences into stepping stones towards success. For this we need a discriminating intellect rooted in the spiritual principles.

One young man had grown up in a spiritual community, yet faced quite a few challenges at an early age. Raised by his mother, he lived in an ashram under the guidance of another guru. He was 16 years old when the guru left his body, and this loss catapulted him into deep sadness. He started to experiment with drugs and plunged into all that the material world had to offer him. Later, he realized that the only thing this destructive way of life could promise him was a feeling of profound emptiness. Still he did not know how to break away from the cycle of drugs and partying that he had embarked upon.

Then his mother took him to meet Amma in London. In the program hall he watched the video about the tsunami, and it changed everything for him. He cried and cried, realizing that he had been wasting his life, while others in the world were dying. He longed to find a way to relieve people of their suffering. When he saw people with video cameras at the program, he thought that perhaps he could work in that department, as he had just completed a course in media technology. Shy to go up to Amma, he kept this thought to himself and did not share it with anyone.

His mother suggested that they attend the program in Ireland at the end of the tour. On the way to the program he met someone who worked in the video department. When they arrived, this man brought him straight up to sit next to Amma. It was translated to Amma that he had some knowledge of video work and wanted to help in some way. Amma suggested that if he wanted to, he could come to India after the European tour had ended. He followed Her suggestion and joined the crew filming Amma in India. He hopes to spend several years traveling with Amma to deepen his foundation in spiritual life, and to resist the temptation to return to his old habits. Amma advises,

> When difficult circumstances arise in life, there are two ways to respond. We can either run away in fear, or kindle the strength from within and try to overcome them. If we choose the first option, all of our strength will be drained and we will be blown about like dry leaves in the wind. It is impossible to escape from some things. One who tries to run away will simply collapse due to exhaustion. Instead, we should gather mental strength, rise up and move to action, spreading the fragrance of selflessness and love. The shadow of fear will only disappear with the dawning of the light of love. Love is our strength. Love is our refuge.

In the early years at the ashram, my seva ranged from cleaning toilets and cutting vegetables, to ironing Amma's clothes. For quite a long time, I also made tea for the construction workers and drinks for the residents. I was never really a tea drinker so, regrettably for everyone, I always made the world's worst tea. The poor workers would often complain about how bad my tea tasted.

One day, I was asked to make tea for Amma. She did not drink it straight away and it went cold, so I heated it up with a little more milk. I was sure it tasted awful, but when a child offers something to the mother with love, then the mother will accept it with love. Amma ended up drinking my terrible concoction and saying how good it was. I knew that She was just trying to be nice to me.

In the beginning days of the ashram, Amma told us not to drink tea or coffee at all. It was known to be bad for spiritual seekers to develop an addiction for it, so we drank a mixture of hot milk and water instead. It was my duty in the early days to make these drinks.

I remember a day when I was praising one of the brahmacharis to Amma, "Amma, that boy, he is not having any sugar in his milk water, isn't that wonderful? What a disciplined person."

Amma did not agree. She said, "Everyone has to have sugar in their milk water!" Because She knew the ego could come from thinking that he was more disciplined than others. She wanted us to always follow the middle path – not too much of something, not too little. Not too little sleep, not too much sleep. Amma is exceedingly practical. Real spirituality is total practicality, as far as Amma is concerned.

As tea was not served in the ashram, some people would go over to Amma's family house to make a tea or coffee for themselves. When She found out about this, She scolded us and said we should no longer do it. But still people would sneak off sometimes to make something to drink. Amma was very angry when She found out about it, so one afternoon we decided to take this matter seriously. All 14 of us went together into the kalari, and it was decided that we all had to promise that we would not drink tea or coffee any more. Each taking turns, we made our vows.

Finally, it got to one person who said, "I promise to *try* not to drink tea or coffee."

Everyone vehemently protested, "No, No, No! You are not allowed to do that; it is not allowed!"

But this particular person said, "I am not going to promise; I am not going to make a vow that I cannot keep." In the end, most of us did make a vow to abstain from caffeine, and we did not drink tea or coffee for many years.

For me, it was nearly 15 years that I kept that vow. Only on rare occasions once or twice a year would I accept a drink that was offered to me so that I would not offend someone's feelings by rejecting it. Until one day, the time came when I started to sit with Amma on the stage for public programs outside of the ashram. I was used to always moving around keeping busy, and when I was suddenly put into the position of having to sit still for a few hours, I found that I began to feel incredibly sleepy. I was very attached to saying, "I don't drink tea or coffee." The ego was boosted from thinking *I am very spiritual because I don't drink caffeine!*

Finally I decided to break my attachment to not drinking caffeine and start drinking a little again, just to keep awake. It was about eight years ago, when we went for a program in Bangalore. I had a small cup of coffee before going onto the stage. It was the first that I had taken for years. While satsang was going on, I could feel a gurgling in my stomach. *O No!* I realized, *I have to go to the bathroom!* I was awake, but I was counting the number of bhajans to go before I could escape. I had forgotten that coffee could act like a strong purgative and diuretic. Five bhajans, four bhajans, three bhajans. Finally, I had to get up and rush off the stage: luckily there was a bathroom close by. I will always remember that first cup of coffee after so many years.

Amma eventually decided that if people were really attached to having tea, they could have it every day. A small amount in a medicinal dose can be okay for us; it is not harmful. Taking just a little keeps us alert, and gives us the energy to keep on going. Amma decided to stop fighting the resistance of those who were sneaking off to have it, and in the end She said everyone should drink tea. This is when chai became incorporated in the daily routine at the ashram. We may forget to think about the *atman* in our daily life by always keeping busy, but we will never forget when it is 4:00 p.m. – chai time!

At one point, someone in the ashram decided to undertake tapas by trying to go without food: eating only a small banana and drinking a glass of milk every evening, nothing else. But this was not very intelligent tapas. It resulted in an ulcer, and in the end required him to eat even more than three meals a day – all because he practiced austerities without using common sense. We must incorporate common sense into our practices; finding moderation in everything is actually the most difficult practice for us to maintain.

A long time ago I kept *maunam* for four months. This meant that I did not speak during that time, which was not terribly difficult. Once one gets into the habit of keeping silence, it becomes a good excuse to avoid problems. When the problems come up, we can motion for that person to "go away," indicating "I am in silence!" However, when one starts to talk again, sometimes it is very difficult to stop.

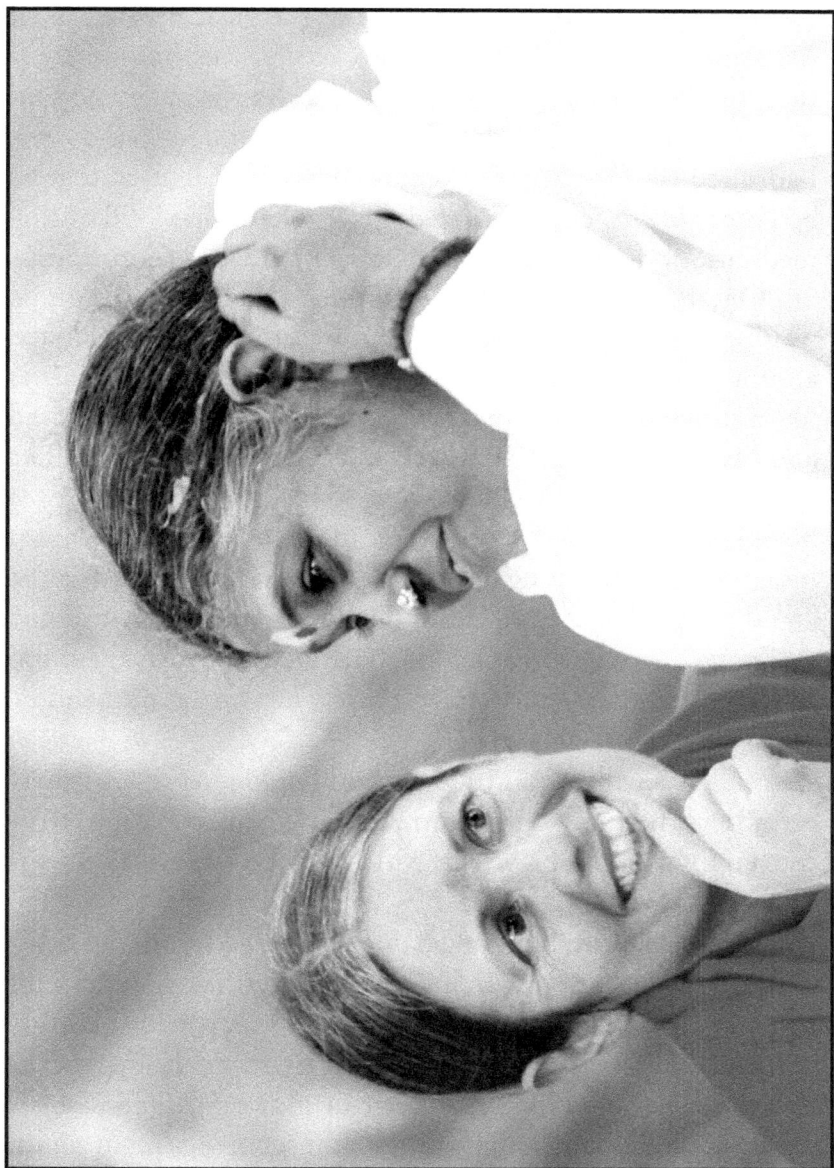

One night, I remember sitting in the kalari during the evening *Devi Bhava* program. One of the great meditators of the ashram was sitting in the back corner meditating. I felt that this person was highly advanced as he was renowned for practicing austerities in the solitude of his underground cave. I admired the intensity of his concentration. I figured that he had probably never experienced the problems that I did during meditation, such as sleepiness and lack of deep absorption.

On this particular evening, I was sitting beside Amma waiting to attend to anything that She might need. I looked around and I noticed that this man was sitting in the corner like a statue. His head was thrust straight back, his eyes closed and his mouth wide open. I felt such a shock seeing him like this. Innocently I thought, *O my goodness! He has attained mahasamadhi and left his body!* Because he was well known for his ability to sit for long hours, it never occurred to me that he could have fallen asleep. Afraid that he was dead, I mentioned to Amma, "I think he has left the body." Amma turned around to look at him and laughed. She threw a candy at him and he woke up – to my great relief.

All of us will see things differently in life. At times it may be difficult to know right from wrong. We must learn to truly use our discrimination wisely, which is not easy and takes years of practice.

A large, heavily-built dog named Sumo had won four competitions as the best dog in his breed. Nevertheless, he and his owners were going to be evicted from the apartment building where they lived, following complaints from the neighbors that the dog snored too loudly. The neighbors insisted that the snoring was so disturbingly loud that it set off alarms at night. The neighbor's father-in-law had a heart condition and could not sleep at night with the unsettling noise. The snoring from the dog was consequently measured, and found to exceed 34 decibels.

The owner of the dog entirely disagreed with the plaintiff saying, "My Sumo is just a young puppy. He sleeps in the bed with me at night, and I don't know why they say he snores that loudly? He does not bother me at all!"

We all have different perceptions about how things in life should be. Our lives are full of us creating our own concepts about everything. That is why it is said that the world is our own projection.

At one time a wealthy man commissioned an author to write his family history, but stipulated that he would have to play down the fact that an uncle had ended a life of crime in the electric chair. He was delighted when the author wrote, "Uncle William occupied a chair of applied electronics in a leading government institution. He was held to the post by the closest of ties and his death came as a real shock."

During English Literature class, a teacher wrote a sentence on the blackboard and said that all the students should try to punctuate it. The sentence was: Woman without her man is nothing.

While all the men punctuated it this way: "Woman, without her man, is nothing." All the women in the class punctuated it like this: "Woman! Without her, man is nothing."

Everyone can choose their own way to view the world. We are incredibly lucky that we have Amma as a spiritual guide to try and refine our way of looking at the world. She thinks of everyone. She would never put us in harm's way or danger. She brings Herself down to our level of consciousness because of Her overwhelming feeling of compassion for suffering people everywhere. But this is not the case with all God-realized masters.

An *Avadhuta* called Prabhakara *Siddha Yogi* lived in Oachira, a little town near the ashram. It was believed that he was 700 years old and that some fishermen pulled him up from the bottom of the ocean in a fishing net.

Avadhutas are individuals who have realized God, who have reached the ultimate state, but act more like crazy people. They live in their own private world of God-intoxication. Although it may seem that they are not so helpful, Amma has said that their breath alone is enough to hold the world in balance. Yet they do not choose to teach disciples in a straightforward way, as Amma does. She has so much compassion to descend to our level to try to guide us – but Avadhutas just stay at their own level of consciousness.

This particular Avadhuta tended to wander around the local areas, but people did not like him coming around. They threw buckets of their dirty water on him because sometimes he grabbed the women. He alleged that it was the desires in the minds of the women that caused him to do this. There were times when he came to visit us in the ashram, usually causing an uproar. People were very protective of the few girls living in the ashram, and warned us to quickly go and lock ourselves inside of a room so that no harm would befall us.

One time we were at a program outside the ashram when he turned up. All of us girls were spending the afternoon outside, behind a grove of trees. Avoiding him also, Amma came to where we were. She explained that Avadhutas have realized God, but people do not understand their actions. She knew that if he did something unusual, people would not understand at all, even though She could appreciate the level where his mind dwelt.

On her way to Amritapuri, the first time she came to India, an American devotee went to Tiruvannamalai to meet an Avadhuta called Yogi Ram Surat Kumar. Hearing he was a God-realized being, she sought him out at the residence his devotees had provided for him. She found him on the porch, which was his darshan area. Carrying a package of dates, she approached him and offered her pranams. Before she had fully risen, he exclaimed, "Amma! Amma! Amma! O Amritanandamayi! That Mother came to visit this beggar! She came and had Her picture taken with this beggar. Amma…" His speech was choked with emotion and in the act of remembering, he seemed to drift into a reverie. The woman was mystified, as she had never met this man before and had no idea how he knew that she was a devotee of Amma.

The following year, she again went to visit him. At one point she asked him a spiritual question. His response was tender but emphatic, "Why are you asking me this question? Why do you ask *me* this question? Your teacher is so great! You are in such good care. You are so protected. O She is so great!" He fully extolled Amma's virtues.

Someone once asked Amma, "What is the greatest sacrifice made by a Mahatma?" Amma replied, "They come to this earth and live among the pigs as pigs and try to uplift them."

People were a little shocked by this, so Amma was quick to add, "Amma was just joking!" But I do not think She was. She was just telling us the truth, which we were not quite ready to hear.

It is the greatest privilege in this lifetime to have the chance to live with a Guru like Amma. Never before has a God-realized soul given so much to the world, as Amma has. An Avadhuta may have the same state of God-realization as a Mahatma. But someone like Amma totally sacrifices that ultimate state of consciousness out of Her compassion and love for us. She is constantly trying to think of new ways to make us happy, to give more of Herself to us, and to uplift us from the shadow of ignorance that clouds our vision and causes us so much sorrow.

Wherever we may be in the world, we have to make the most of where God has placed us. Even if we live in the midst of a busy material world, it does not matter what we do, we cannot say that only *this* is spiritual and *that* is worldly. For Amma, who really knows the Truth, there is no difference. She sees God in all of creation, so what can be said to be worldly? If we perform good actions, then grace will definitely flow to us wherever we may be.

People may complain that daily life is more challenging for them because they live far away from Amma. They project that somehow their problems will simply vanish if they could live in Amma's physical presence. We should not waste time feeling sorry for ourselves, but instead should make some effort to hold on to the essence of Amma's Universal love and compassion and try to do something good for others, in whatever way we can. Then surely the grace that flows to us, will guide us through the journey of life.

Chapter 13

Tsunami Angels

Life's most urgent question is:
What are you doing for others?
Martin Luther King Jr.

In the summer of 2003, Amma had given a warning that a tremendous natural disaster could soon occur. She said that we could not stop this from happening. All we could do was pray and try to perform good actions.

Amma's followers started to prepare for the difficulty that would come about in the future. Some took all of their money out of the stock market, purchased gold or moved to different locations. Others felt that the safest thing to do was to spend as much time as they could with Amma at Amritapuri.

Recently, Amma laughed mischievously remembering that a great many people had come to be with Her in India to try to escape the predicted catastrophe. Instead, the ashram in India is *exactly* where the tsunami struck.

Fortunately, Amma's protection was full and complete. Absolutely no one out of at least 18,000 devotees here on that day was hurt. It was heart-breaking to come into contact with the death and destruction that struck all around the ashram. Yet Amma's all-encompassing love totally surrounded us. Due to Amma's powerful grace, some people had the most profound experiences of their lives.

At the time the tsunami hit the coast of Kerala, the ashram was filled to capacity with foreign visitors. For many, ashram life is already challenging, with modest accommodation and food. But with the tsunami, all the residents and visitors of the ashram were evacuated to the Amrita University buildings across the backwaters. This was relatively a small inconvenience – in comparison with the tragic loss that surrounded us. Local villagers had lost their homes, their belongings and in a lot of cases at least one of their immediate family members if not more.

Villagers, residents and visitors were all evacuated together to the mainland across the backwaters. Everyone had to make do with only the clothes they had on their backs at the time of the tsunami. Amongst all the discomfort and deprivation, we were living like refugees. Sleeping in classrooms and hallways, any space that could be found. But still everyone tried to remain light-hearted.

It was easier to leave behind the need for comfort when we thought of the local villagers who suffered such incredible losses. Instead of focusing on what we were missing, people sought ways to help – chopping vegetables; serving food to the villagers; volunteering at the hospital and consoling those who were deeply grieving. In this service of others, the visitors and residents of the ashram fulfilled Amma's wish that we should light the lamps of love in our hearts to ease the suffering of others.

That historic night, a group of American women were trying to fall asleep on the bare concrete. One woman lay directly on the ground and pulled a straw sleeping mat over her like a blanket. She realized that this must be similar to how the homeless who sleep in cardboard boxes must feel. She looked over and saw the person next to her using her large padded bra for a comfortable pillow. This woman felt extremely proud of the industrious use of her clothing, until someone else started to laugh, claiming that actually she should win the prize for the most ingenious creation for a pillow. Hers consisted of a pair of long underwear that a man had been wearing for three days. As a great sacrifice on his part, he had generously given his long johns to her. Laughter was the guiding force that carried these people through the difficult times.

When Amma gave Her acceptance speech at the 2006 Interfaith Center of New York Awards Program, She stated that we should all try to become role models to inspire others to do good actions. An Australian devotee did an excellent job of becoming an extraordinary inspiration for a lot of us. I will always think of this young woman as one of the tsunami angels, even though in her humility she does not like to be referred to as such.

In her second year of medical school in Australia, she was spending a holiday in Thailand with a friend when the tsunami hit. She had been staying in the fourth row of bungalows on the beach. The first three rows were completely wiped out by the wave. Grace saved her right from the beginning.

She was distressed to wake up hearing terrifying screams on what was supposed to be a joyous time, the day after Christmas. After a night of celebration, she suddenly found the world turned upside down. Her roommate ran into the room crying hysterically. She had seen a huge wave headed straight towards them. A deafening noise filled the room as if a plane was dropping bombs on them. She did not know if she was dreaming, or just still a little tipsy from the previous night. What she did know, was that she had never felt more frightened in her whole life.

After their bungalow and their nerves had the life shaken out of them, they opened the door. Water completely surrounded them. The front steps of the bungalow were gone and the entire contents of the restaurant and tourist office were floating around them. Computers, clothes, speakers and backpacks – what was once the livelihood and all the desires of people – floated by in the rushing water. Paradise island turned into a nightmare. Instantly, things were put into perspective.

The survivors were evacuated to higher ground and after a few hours were allowed to come down again. After this, the two young Australian women went off to see what they could do to help. The places where they had walked a few days before, were now unrecognizable. Boats perched in trees and concrete pavements stuck out vertically. Bodies were scattered here and there amidst the rubble from building materials and shattered glass that covered the ground. They visited the hospital to look for their friends but could not find them anywhere. The next step was the morgue.

The morgue, overfilled with decomposing bodies, was in utter chaos and confusion. They decided to help there, as it desperately needed a better system to cope with the overload of dead bodies. With some of the bodies decomposing so badly, it was a horrible situation that very few were willing to deal with. People who visited the morgue in an attempt to identify bodies of their loved ones, found absolutely no support, aside from the small collection of volunteers. Most of the helpers left after the first day as they could not stand the smell and shocking sights inside the morgue. One of the girls felt too squeamish to work inside with all the bodies, so put her efforts into helping people on the outside

The other girl stayed, working 12 or more hours each day helping families to file reports describing their lost loved ones. They noted objects and markings that might still be recognizable, like jewelry, tattoos, piercings or scars. She collected the information and then searched through the bodies with the hopes of a positive identification. She waited for the new shipment of bodies that had been recovered and were delivered in the evenings. She looked through them after the forensic team had finished. That way she would get to the bodies first and identify them, so the families did not have to see the horror

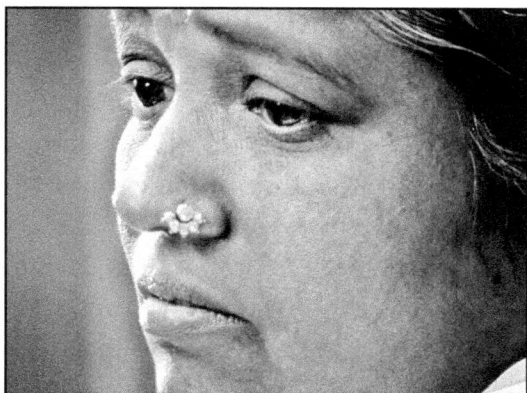

of their decomposing faces. It was such a dreadful place, not a place where anyone would want to find their loved one.

The forensic doctors treated her kindly as they respected what she was trying to do. Although at times they made jokes about her being the lowest in the food chain, as she often had to ask for a knife to scrape off dead skin and maggots to prepare a body to be seen by the family. But she did not care; no one else was going to do it.

It was very traumatic work, and each minute of the day she experienced more horror than what most people have to see in a lifetime. She said that only the memory of Amma gave her the strength to be able to carry on.

Knowing the mental anguish and pain of the families that came to seek their loved ones' remains, she tried as much as possible to spare them any more pain than they had already suffered. Besides helping to identify the bodies, she also tried to comfort and give solace to the people. She sometimes took them out for coffee or simply tried to give them emotional support.

After a few months of working there, she had to return to Australia as her money had totally run out. It was no surprise that after spending so many hours surrounded by decaying bodies, maggots, heat and phenomenal grief, she had a vastly different perspective on life. She arrived home feeling very much out of place. She felt like a stranger in the place she had once called home. She was disgusted with the futility of it all, "I bought a new skirt"… "John cheated on Sarah…" She became very restless back in Australia because she knew of the tremendous suffering of people in other places.

She did not have any more funds to travel and decided to give her story to a newspaper in return for just enough money to purchase an airline ticket to Sri Lanka. She then flew to Sri Lanka with her brother and they both worked together helping the tsunami victims as much as they could.

On one occasion in Sri Lanka, a man turned up with a large bleeding cut on his head. The local doctor refused to treat him, and although she had never stitched a wound before, she knew the necessity of doing it right then and there, before he lost too much blood. She courageously attempted the first few stitches and then successfully finished the job that even local doctors were hesitant to undertake.

She was nominated for the Young Australian Award for Bravery. Humanitarians from all over the world were touched with pride and wonder at her great courage and selfless nature. Although she did not win first prize for the award, she is considered the winner in many hearts.

Another kind-hearted angel also felt the urge to help in Sri Lanka during the aftermath of the tsunami. As so much of the island was devastated, bodies were just left on the beach to rot. After seeing the unclaimed body of a small girl lying on the beach, this man decided that he would collect her body and put it to rest, looking upon her as his little sister. Lovingly he picked up her body and buried her with the same kind of care as he would have given someone in his own family. He continued to remove the other bodies in the same way, seeing each of them as his family.

He lived without food for long stretches of time, doing this work simply to help. Finally the locals realized the impact and sincerity of his actions and they took it upon themselves to feed him whatever they could.

He wanted to organize the chanting of *Om Namah Shivaya* because he knew the people deeply needed spiritual consolation at that time. Although threatened with murder from the local militant group, he repeated that he was not afraid of death. He said that they could kill him if they wanted to but he was going to arrange for the chanting come what may – and he did. Needless to say, once they realized his courage and strength of character they let him do just as he wanted.

Both of these young people totally forgot themselves in their desire to do something good for others in need. Their simple heroic actions make this selfish world a much better place.

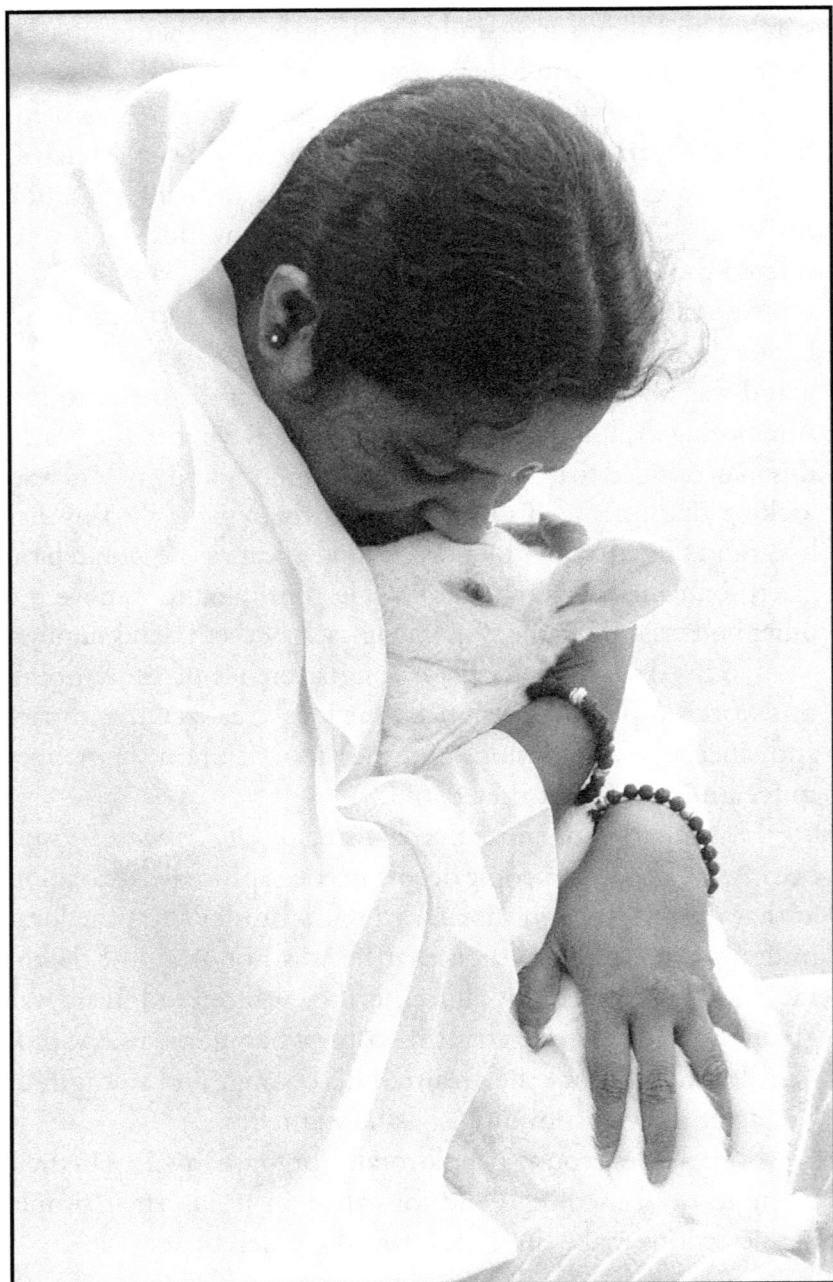

Amma's inspiration gives us the strength to achieve tremendous things when we are guided by a selfless attitude. In that time of great suffering and sorrow after the tsunami, not only people, but also animals wanted to help each other.

In Nairobi, a baby hippopotamus survived the tsunami's waves on the Kenyan coast. It weighed 300 kilos, yet still it was swept down a river into the Indian Ocean, then again forced back to shore with the tumultuous wave. After it lost its mother, the hippo was traumatized. It was taken to a wildlife preserve and ended up being mothered by a giant century-old tortoise. They developed such a strong bond with each other: the tortoise took the role of a foster mother and let the hippo follow it around as if it was its own child. The two ate, slept and swam together like mother and child.

A seven-year-old boy was saved from the tsunami's force by the family dog that pulled the boy up a hill and out of the small hut where he had taken shelter. The boy's mother had fled with her two younger children, hoping that her older boy would be strong enough to outrun the wave on his own. When the boy ran into the hut, the dog nudged him back outside and up a nearby hill.

In times of fear and sorrow, love and compassion go beyond all boundaries. At one time I noticed a small newspaper cutting about a young, hard-working government officer. He was telling how he had gained a lot of his disaster management experience while dealing with a terrible fire tragedy that had happened in Kumbhakonam, near Chennai.

In that accident, 94 small school children had been burnt to death, and those who survived were badly injured. Some of the parents had even lost two of their children in the fire. We cannot even imagine their sorrow or how they were able to face the future after this kind of suffering. The government officer went on to tell, with tears in his eyes, that during the tsunami relief operations that he was conducting, he was again able to meet some of the mothers of these children.

All of the parents got together and although most of them were very poor themselves, they worked hard to collect the equivalent of $2,500, and came to offer the money to him for tsunami relief. They were women who had lost their children in the fire – giving money for children who had lost their parents in the tsunami.

Sorrow had become their guide, leading them towards opening their hearts.

During the time of the tsunami, dirty water and mud flooded through all the ground floor rooms of the ashram at Amritapuri. Many things in my storeroom were destroyed or slightly spoiled. After we had gone through and cleaned and sorted everything, I found a lot of different old beads that I thought were too ugly to make anything out of. They were useless to me.

I set aside the worst of these, thinking that I could give them to the small children at the tsunami relief camps. I imagined that they could amuse themselves making necklaces from them. I waited for some time till I found a girl who was willing to take these supplies off to the camp to give to the children. The girl later related to me what happened when she took them to one of the smallest relief camps that was situated near the ashram.

She said that the people took out some plastic mats to sit and work on, then they spread all of the beads and supplies out and started to sort them. I had also given some fishing line to thread them on and some old clasps that I had no use for.

The people sat there for several hours in silence, carefully stringing together what turned into beautiful necklaces. Contrary to what I had thought, it was not the women and children that came to do this beading work; it was mostly the men. They had so much fun, working with concentration to produce something beautiful out of another person's waste. A few of the men adorned themselves with the necklaces, and they all enjoyed laughing with each other at how funny they looked.

It was a wonderful chance to be able to bring joy to these tough fishermen who had lost so much. They revealed that they felt helpless because they could not provide food, clothes or shelter for their families any more – if they had any family left.

Amma understood that these fishermen knew no other work but to make their living from the sea. She felt that if they did not work for a few months that they could become suicidal with the frustration of thinking that they had become useless.

To bring a smile to the faces of the women and children had not been so difficult, and through this exercise the men also found a chance to smile and to experience joy again. Meanwhile, Amma was also building a new fleet of fishing boats for them.

In India, the tsunami caused the greatest amount of damage in the state of Tamil Nadu. Amma immediately sent out brahmacharis to start relief work there, providing the displaced people with food and temporary housing until permanent homes could be constructed. The ashram distributed rice and other dry goods to thousands. Someone showed Amma photographs of the locals receiving these basic provisions. I looked over Her shoulder while She was going through the photos and I will never forget one of them. It showed a man crying, holding a large plastic bag. The brahmachari was trying to comfort him. This man had a bag of rice, but no one to cook it for him and no family to share it with, as all of his family had died during the tsunami. I will always remember the look of unbearable grief on his face.

In the village near Amritapuri, countless families were devastated because their relatives or children died in the tsunami. Some women were able to become pregnant again, but others had undergone tubal ligation surgery and were totally distraught to have lost their children, with no chance to have more. A few of these women had even lost two children.

When Amma heard of the plight of these unfortunate families, She researched the possibility for reversal operations to provide the women with a chance for conception again. Amma insisted that the doctors utilize the best technology possible for these reconstructive surgeries. Six women underwent this procedure and one of them successfully conceived. A healthy baby was born to an infinitely grateful couple.

When Amma learned that the recanalization procedures had not been successful for the others, She advised the doctors at AIMS to research in-vitro fertilization. Three women underwent this procedure and became pregnant. One of them, who had lost both a daughter and a son, gave birth to twins – a boy and a girl. Her family has been restored through Amma's compassion and grace. These newborns could be called the true angels of the tsunami. Amma gave these women life once more, and the chance for them to smile again, one of the biggest miracles of all.

Chapter 14

Forgetting Ourselves

*When a person responds to the joys and sorrows
of others as if they were their own, they have
attained the highest state of spirituality.*
Bhagavad Gita 6:32

The love of a true mother is incomparable. Her endurance and perseverance are unsurpassed. She forgets herself, not thinking at all of her own physical body, always putting the thought of her children before her own needs. Sometimes she may even sacrifice her own food and sleep for the sake of her child, but still she is happy because she is doing all of this out of love for the child.

Amma tells a story of how vast a mother's love can be. It is a story from Tamil Nadu, of a great queen's love and sacrifice for the world. The queen was coming close to giving birth to her child, so she called an astrologer to predict the child's future. The astrologer foretold that if the baby was born at a certain time it would bring a lot of harm to her, the king and also to the kingdom. But if the child was born at a later period, then the child would be illustrious, kind and generous and would bring a lot of good fortune to the kingdom.

The queen was very aware of the dates that she had been given for the auspicious birth time. Unfortunately, she started to develop labor pains very early. She started to think, *If I deliver the baby now, it will bring misfortune to the whole kingdom. I should never allow this to happen.* The queen gave her maid orders to hang her upside down so the birth of the child would be delayed. She remained like this until the auspicious time arrived when she had been told that the child should be born.

When this time came, she asked the maid to cut her down so she could give birth to the child. Due to the extreme trauma, the queen did not survive. However, as a result of his mother's incredible sacrifice, her son later became a great saint.

There is nothing more powerful than a mother's love. During the tsunami in Thailand, when everyone panicked and ran away in terror from the roaring wave, a Swedish woman ran in the opposite direction from everyone else, straight into the huge wave. She was photographed sprinting into the water, trying to save her husband, brother and three sons. Afterwards, newspapers reported that no one knew whether the mother or her family had survived. Later this woman who had run into the wave saw the newspaper article and reported that her entire family survived and that they were all reunited soon after the water had carried them to higher ground. After coming so close to death, they realized how precious life is and how strong the love of a mother can be, to risk her own life to save others. The purity and selflessness of a mother's love will always give her the strength needed to do anything.

If someone is drowning and we want to save them, then we cannot have any concern for ourselves at that time. We have to melt away our own ego in order to be able to try and save another. In this same way, if we really love God within, then we too can totally forget ourselves. We should strive for this kind of love. This is the type of love that Amma feels for the world. It gives Her the strength to go on and on and on, endlessly receiving people.

Sometimes when people go for Amma's darshan, in their enthusiasm to come into Her embrace they lunge at Her, step on Her feet, and may even physically hurt Her. They demand so many things from Her, and still She will treat every single one of those people's concerns as if coming from Her very own children. Maybe we could only sit for a half hour listening to the same kind of questions over and over before we would finally jump up and run away. But Amma, sits patiently, paying attention to everyone who comes to Her. She uplifts aching hearts and listens to problems for hours and hours on end, even while Her own body may be hurting. Thinking nothing of Her own comfort, She sees to everyone else first and Herself last.

Amma is the perfect example of absolute self-control. Sometimes we may feel that we have reached our limit. But often when we are pushed to the point that we think is our limit, we may find we can still go further. For Amma, there are no limits or boundaries. She always gives the maximum of Herself in every situation no matter how She may be feeling. Amma's love gives Her the power and the ability to do anything.

We can try our best to follow Her example, but usually find ourselves unable to do so. Our minds trick us into thinking that perhaps we should take a little more rest, or that we should save our strength as we are not feeling well. But not Amma. She offers Her every breath only for the world, and never has a thought for Herself. She is an example of absolute compassion and absolute forgiveness. Perhaps that explains why many people think of Her as the "Absolute."

161

In 2003 we had to cancel the Australian tour due to the difficulty of traveling with a large group during the *SARS* crisis. At this time I received a letter from one of the satsang group organizers. She wrote:

> I have been very involved in assisting with the arrangements for the Tour. Needless to say, I, like so many others, am grieving at this time, as we long so much to see Amma when She is not with us.
>
> I know that Amma knows the thoughts and feelings of all Her children and that She is thinking of us strongly, and She is feeling sad about not coming. From my own point of view, I would wish that Amma should also know that Her children, although grieving, have through Her grace, risen with a positive strength to meet this circumstance. It has been through Her grace alone that so much love, cooperation, efficiency and opening of hearts has taken place, and continues to do so.
>
> My tears flow, not through sadness, but through gratitude, which I cannot adequately put into words…I just want to fall at Her blessed feet again and again.
>
> It is completely awe-inspiring that Amma can at the same time have such a combination of motherly concern for each individual and universal insight, which encompasses the past, present and future.
>
> It has been a most blessed gift to see this, at whatever low level I am able to understand it. This is truly Amma's sweetest prasad, and I will remember to try so much harder to behave in a dharmic way in my

everyday dealings in life, because my Amma, who
is the Architect of the Law, chooses to behave as an
example of perfection for Her children.

How lucky we are to be able to consider ourselves
Amma's children, and to be able to serve Her, and
begin to learn however falteringly, to walk in Her
holy footsteps.

We have a choice in life. We can either suffer, or accept
unfortunate circumstances as God's will like these people did.
Although they were completely devastated that Amma did not
visit them that year, they totally forgot about their personal
desires in an act of surrender.

When the heart opens with love to embrace everything
– even the adverse situations – as God's will, then grace truly
flows to us.

While some people feel happy to have found a deeper
attachment to Amma, others may worry that this may not
be good for them. They think that they should become more
independent and free, and do not entirely understand the feeling of painful longing that they sometimes start to experience
in growing closer to Amma.

Our minds always need to cling to something. When we
are a small child we hold on tightly to our mother and father.
As we grow older, we want to spend a lot of time with our
friends, and when we get married, we depend on our husband
or wife. The nature of the mind is to always want something
to hold onto for support. Amma offers Herself as a stairway to
climb to God-realization. Attachment to Amma is truly only
to guide us to the highest state, because we cannot reach this
Supreme state on our own.

One young woman felt she needed to spend more time with Amma every year. She was not very comfortable with this feeling of neediness, as she put it, as it was so foreign to the conditioning that she had been brought up within the West. She told Amma how she felt, and Amma responded, "Amma likes your innocence, and with your pure resolve all these things will come true. In the beginning, devotion is difficult. It begins like a river and eventually becomes like the ocean. And one day there will be no separation between you and the ocean."

This young woman shared how she felt after talking to Amma about her doubts:

> I have found so much solace in Her words. Amma told me to come closer. What I see is that She was telling me I am still developing, I am still a child and need to be close to my Mother while I am becoming more attached to God and less attached to the world. The neediness I was feeling was progress not regression. In order to replace attachment to the world with attachment to Her, I need to be close to Her. But as I grow more firmly attached to God I won't need to be close to Her physical form because I will have merged within Her.
>
> The sense of attachment is counterintuitive to Western thinking. It feels like regression because we have a steady conditioning of thinking that independence is what makes you grown up, mature and responsible. But we are never independent; we are dependent on the world to satisfy our desires and that makes us miserable. My Western mind still judges, saying that I am regressing, that I need to

find God within, and why can't I just meditate and feel that? My attachment to Amma has helped me to be less attached to things in the world that don't serve me. She's literally replacing those attachments.

Some people find themselves through devotion, while others lose themselves in it completely.

While traveling through the state of Karnataka we stayed the night at Amma's school at Karwar. The local people were very excited at the thought of Amma's program. They were bubbling over with devotion. Police lined up to keep the crowd from rushing towards Amma as She made Her way to the vehicle to go to the program. With the overwhelming devotion rising in the crowd, the police forgot that it was their duty to stop the mob of people from surging towards Amma. The police themselves became the first to rush forward to touch Amma's feet. In a reversal of roles, I had to be the police person, and started pulling them off of Amma so we could make our way through.

At Ahmedabad in 2006, a family accompanied by a very sick old woman came to seek Amma's blessing. The elderly woman could not walk or talk and was sustained on a feeding tube. Her brother asked Amma to cure her. He said that for the last three months she had been immobile and had lost the capacity to talk. Her family had carried her to Amma in a chair, as the woman was almost in a vegetative state. Amma had visited their house some years before, so the family brought her to see Amma in the hope of awakening something inside of her through devotion.

Amma called out to the aged woman a few times. Gradually she started to recognize Amma's voice and slowly came back to life. She moaned happily and began moving her arms, trying to touch Amma's lips and face. Tears came from her eyes and also her brother's eyes, as he was overwhelmed with gratitude to Amma. The few of us around nearly cried too. It was deeply moving to see someone in an almost comatose state coming back to life in recognizing Amma.

One year later, the family brought her to see Amma again. She was in a wheelchair this time. As she was brought into the room her face brightened with excitement. She reached out her hands to touch Amma's smiling face. She was not really able to talk, but with concentrated effort she managed to squeeze four words out, which she repeated several times to the joy of everyone. She slowly started to mouth, "Amma…I…love… you." We all were so happy to see the vast improvement in her health from last year. Her family told that after seeing Amma the previous year she had steadily improved and was not on any kind of medication at all. Love for Amma kept her going. No matter how young or old, everyone is a child in the eyes of that Motherly love.

One devotee in Los Angeles worked diligently to help prepare for the annual program and so was offered a special treat because of all his hard work. The organizers asked him if he wanted to put Amma's shoes on. (Someone usually holds Amma's shoes at the end of the program, and helps Her into them.) In deep thought, he took quite a while to answer. We wondered why he did not quickly take up the offer. Finally he replied, "They won't fit me, will they?"

Afterwards we laughed for a long time when he explained that he thought that maybe he was being offered the chance to wear Amma's shoes for a little while to soak up all the positive energy from them.

One man always loved to meditate and had participated in many different retreats, but he says his best meditation was when he got the chance to do selfless service at the first Malaysian program in 2002.

During the two days of programs, the tour group traveling with Amma literally worked around the clock with no rest and hardly any food or water. Yet offering themselves in this way seemed to bring the best out of everyone. There was hardly time for a selfish thought – everyone was willing to do whatever they could to help.

With such a tremendous crowd of thousands meeting Amma for the first time, most people had to wait in the hot sun for hours before they received their darshan. On the second day, there were over 500 special needs families, children in wheel chairs and hundreds of elderly people. The hall was far too small to accommodate the huge crowd, so we worked consistently to help arrange a space out of the sun where the special needs families could wait for their turn to have darshan.

The group traveling with Amma served enthusiastically at the programs and never felt any real hardship. This seemed to be Amma's grace, for them to work so hard and feel incredibly fulfilled with little comfort or rest time. Some of them only saw Amma twice during the two days of programs, when She called for them to hand the prasad to Her for five minutes each during the darshan. However, working in the bookstore and trying to help manage the crowds, people said that they have never felt closer to Amma. Forgetting themselves in the act of service brought them more peace of mind than any kind of meditation ever had.

In finding Amma within and forgetting ourselves while serving Her, we discover the possibility of knowing real freedom and happiness. What we gain is immeasurable and what we lose or forget is nothing but that which separates us from our true Selves.

When asked by reporters what Amma experiences when She embraces people during darshan, Amma responded that She becomes one with them, experiencing their pains, sorrows and joys. She sees others as She sees Her own face in the mirror. She no longer sees two, but only sees one. Through the act of selfless love we all become one.

Chapter 15

True Surrender

If sparks fly,
I shall think my thirst and hunger quelled.
If the sky tears down,
I shall think it pouring for my bath.
If a hillside slides on me,
I shall think it flowers for my hair.
O Lord white as jasmine,
if my head falls from my shoulders,
I shall think it your offering.
                                    Mahadevi akka

When people try to praise Amma for all She does, She never wants to take the credit for anything. In Her astounding humility, She says that She is just an instrument. She says She has so many good children and that is how all of the wonderful projects are accomplished. Amma says that She is just like a pipe that channels from the Source.

In 1987, when we embarked upon the very first World Tour, I always wondered how things would turn out. I knew that we loved Amma but what would people in the West feel? I worried a little about how people would perceive Her, because I had seen so many extraordinary facets of Amma's Divine nature.

The Holy Mother aspect was only one of the myriad of faces that She showed to us. She could also become like an innocent child, a crazy woman and also the form of Kali, trying to destroy our ego. Amma would become whatever we needed to help us break out of the rigid shell of our likes and dislikes. She could strike fear in us when our mistakes were being corrected, as well as melt our unyielding hearts with just one compassionate glance. Amma did not speak much English and always dressed in traditional Indian clothing, so I wondered if people in the West were ready to accept Her. I doubted whether they would be able to fully recognize Amma's greatness, so deeply hidden in Her humility.

We found Amma absolutely irresistible, but the world had never seen another spiritual Master quite like Her. Of course, my silly thoughts were absolutely unfounded. Amma never had any doubts about being accepted. She was always completely surrendered to God's will and instructed us never to worry about anything, that God would always provide.

Amma has never allowed anyone to ask for anything in Her name. She has always wanted us to work hard to achieve whatever was needed. Right from the very beginning, when people first came to Her to unburden their sorrows, God's grace and destiny has unfolded.

In the early days of the ashram, there were just a few thatched huts to live in, although often we would sleep outside on the sand, under the stars. Our sparse accommodation was sometimes offered to visitors who came and had no other place to stay. At one point, a devotee gave some money to build a prayer hall. Around the same time, Amma heard of the sad plight of the children at the Paripally orphanage that was in such terrible condition. With the money intended for the hall construction, She decided to buy the orphanage to relieve the children of their dreadful living conditions. We had to wait a few more years for the hall to be built, but She knew that we would always manage.

Sometimes when we ran short of a basic necessity, we would start to panic and worry about how to be able to purchase more, as there was no money available to do so. Just at the moment when we started to get really anxious, someone would turn up offering a small donation that exactly covered the amount needed. Later, we always realized how ridiculous our worry had been. God was always looking after us.

Amma says that She always knew that She was destined to become as She is. Fully aware of Her inner nature from birth, She realized that She was supposed to offer Herself to serve the world. I think it is God's grace that gives Her the strength to serve the people, to do what She has to do. It defies medical history that She is able to go on as She does.

Most of the great Saints who came before, suffered from some kind of illness or disease, but still they served the people, even while suffering. They did not shut themselves away in a room or not see people due to illness. They conveyed the lesson that even with hardship still we should go beyond it to serve. We should just keep on giving to others.

One of Amma's greatest teachings is in observing Her life. She has the formidable self-control to put Herself completely above the consciousness of Her own body. Sometimes during a late program when we are all ready to go home and get some sleep, Amma will slow everything down and give the best darshans to those who come last. Her body may be in pain, but She goes beyond it and totally forgets Herself. She wants it to be like that, for She has given Herself as a gift to the world and says that a gift once given should never be taken back.

A beautiful story illuminates how the Mahatmas keep on giving to the world. They cannot help themselves – it is simply their nature to give. Their hearts are filled with so much love that they overflow with compassion. Even if the world does not understand what they are doing, their nature compels them to keep on giving and giving.

Once there was a Mahatma who was born to a very low caste. He was a potter by profession and although he had attained Self-realization, he continued to do his pottery work. Daily he went into the forest, making use of clay and the potter's wheel to produce ten pots. He spent the rest of his time in meditation. He tried to give the pots that he made to the villagers but because he belonged to the lowest caste, nobody would accept charity from him.

One day he developed a plan. He went to each house saying that he had come to sell the pots. He announced, "I have ten pots for sale. Are you interested in buying them? Each pot costs 15 rupees." This angered the people in the house because they knew that the cost of the pot should only be around ten rupees. They told the potter that they did not want his pots because they could buy them elsewhere for less. They commanded him to leave and to take all of the pots with him.

The potter said, "Okay, you don't have to buy them. I will take my nine pots back," even though he had actually given ten pots. The person in the house then thought, *He doesn't know how many pots he has given me. Maybe I can keep that one extra pot myself because he doesn't realize that he is missing it.* The potter went from one house to another and left a pot behind in each household. The people never realized that he was purposely giving the pots to them.

In the same way, God always gives to us even when we think we do not want or even need that grace. We can never comprehend exactly how a perfect Master is working on us to try to bring us away from our self-inflicted suffering. Our limited mind and intellect cannot perceive more than a fraction of what they are really able to give us.

One of Amma's American devotees found in Amma what she had always been searching for: a loving mother and a spiritual guide who could lead her from darkness to light. She realized that only the grace from a spiritual guide could fill in all the gaps in her life and make it complete. One night during a program at the San Ramon ashram, she was talking to a friend who was volunteering with parking seva. Suddenly they were interrupted by a woman who rushed up and announced, "One of your guys up on the meditation hillside needs help!"

Her friend reached for a walkie-talkie to call the security section and ask them to go up there. In the meantime, her friend casually said to her, "Why don't you go up there and take a look at what's going on?"

The woman agreed and made her way out the door and on up the hill. She had been given a lollipop earlier that day, and happened to have this in her mouth while walking up the hill.

As there was no moon at all, it was fairly dark and she could not see very well. To her left, in the bushes she saw what appeared to be a pile of clothes. She walked closer to the pile of clothes and heard a voice coming from them, "Hey, can you give me a hand?" It was an Australian man who worked as a part of the security team at that time.

She walked a little closer to the pile of clothes and as her eyes started to adjust to the darkness, she realized that the pile of clothes was actually two men. The Australian security man was on his back and another person was sitting on top of him, pinning him to the ground.

When she finally realized what was going on, she immediately began to pull this fellow off of the other one. The young man began to struggle. To prevent him from jumping on her, she briskly threw him to the ground, face down, and grabbed his right arm, pinning it behind his back in an arm lock. He was still struggling to get to his feet, but she did not let him get up, increasing the grip that she had on him. She was not at all angry or perturbed, but simply kept him tightly under control. She was actually afraid that she might hurt him if he did not stop struggling.

After a few minutes the other security man showed up. He leapt onto the fellow and restrained him from the other side. After this, the young man settled down, completely exhausted. The two Australian security men turned towards her with big grins on their faces. At first she did not know if they were smiling at the fact that a woman had rescued one of them, or if it was due to the fact that she still had the lollipop in her mouth – or maybe it was both. Through the whole ordeal, that lollipop never left her mouth. She actually finished the lollipop after they had all stood up.

Afterward, she never personally went up to Amma to tell Her about the experience because she thought her ego would get inflated. But very quickly, the story went around about how a girl had saved the strong Australian men. Amma thought it was wonderful that a female had saved them, and in the end She told a hilarious version of the story to others: A girl was

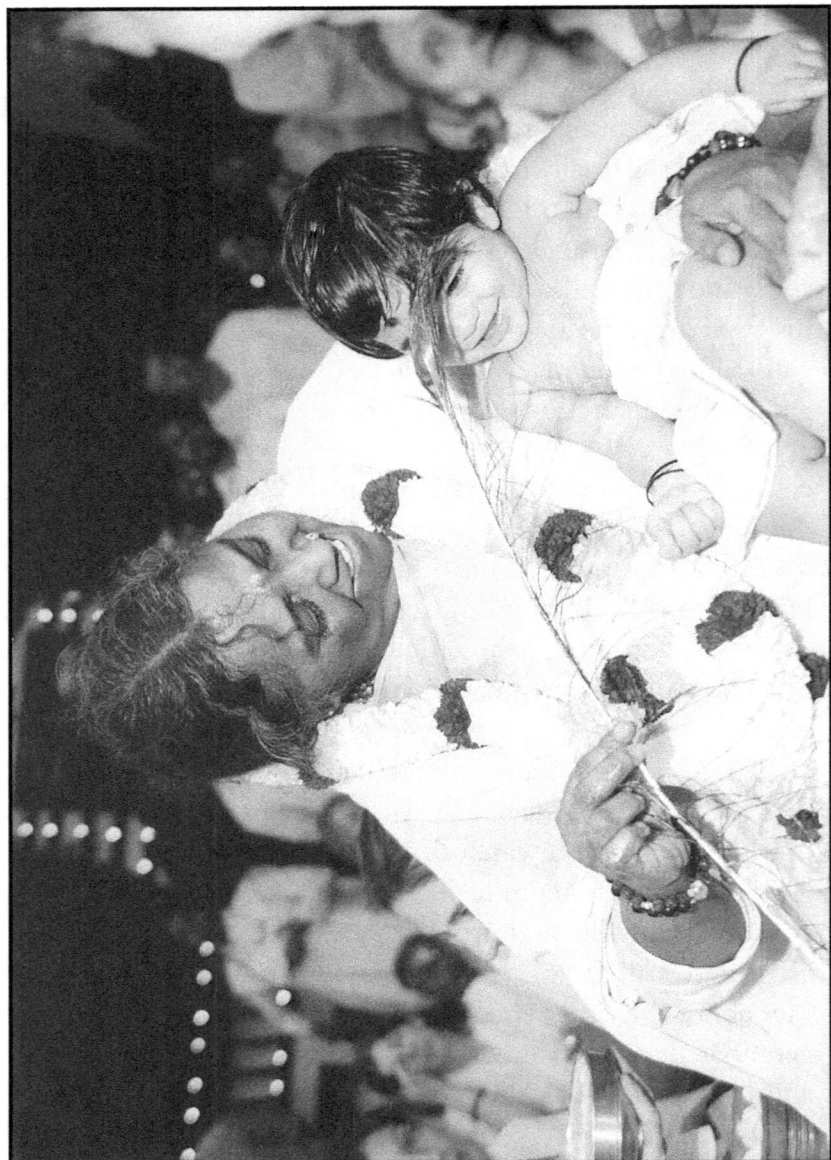

casually walking up the hill with a lollipop in her mouth; she saw a crazy man fighting with the men; she walked up to the crazy man and hit him with her lollipop and the crazy man went flying.

In San Ramon, a very nice woman gave her a paper award, the Lollipop Hero award. She thought that Amma would have a good laugh again out of seeing it, so she carried this award with her in the hopes of eventually showing it to Amma.

On the very last day of the tour, the tour staff had a picnic with Amma in Boston right before She was to leave for India. While Amma was busy serving everyone their plates of food, she showed her award to Amma.

Amma asked the Australian man to tell the story of how he had been rescued. When he finished, Amma took the award in Her hand and began to tell a story of Her own:

> "There was a fire, and it was so big and strong, that it had grown completely out of control. All the fire trucks were afraid to go near it. Extra fire trucks came from all over, but none would dare go into it. Suddenly out of nowhere this one fire truck rushed straight into the fire. This gave all the other fire trucks courage and they followed straight behind. Soon they were able to put out the fire. Proud of the bravery of the first fire truck driver, the others wanted to give him an award. They set up a big banquet on his behalf and when everyone was there to show their appreciation, they asked him if there was anything that they could do for him to show their gratitude. He replied, "I would like the brakes on my fire truck fixed!""

Everyone laughed. Amma then held up the paper award and said, "Is that what her award is for?" No one said a word. The Lollipop Hero started to get really nervous. Her mind raced back to that evening and she began questioning her actions on that night. Then Amma turned to the Australian man and said, "I asked you to tell your side of the story. The fire truck story was meant for you!" She then imitated the woman sucking on her lollipop. She rolled Her eyes back and forth like a child, and then pretended to hit the bad guy with the lollipop. Amma and everyone else laughed uproariously. She looked at the award for quite some time with a big smile on Her face, then announced to everyone how courageous this woman had been. Amma kissed her on the top of her head and handed her back the award.

This woman knew that she had just been an instrument in the hands of the Master. She had taken action but her mind had been totally calm and present with no fears, anxieties or worries. She had not been thinking of the future and what might happen, nor had she been paralyzed from memories of the past, unable to act. She had just been there responding to help, just in the moment. To believe that she had been the doer would have been a big mistake. She had heard before that when one achieves something great, it is truly the grace of the Guru.

When she thought about it later, this woman realized the lollipop was the real hero of the story, for the lollipop symbolizes child-like innocence. The fact that she never let go of that lollipop, or should it be said that the lollipop never let go of her, was the real message. In that true state of innocence and of leaving the ego behind, the Guru's grace will always save us and others too.

Amma reminds us that on this journey we are never alone. God is always with us. The love and light of the Supreme is always guiding us, but we should allow God to hold our hand. For this to happen we must have self-surrender. When we have self-surrender, grace will certainly flow to us and we will ultimately find true happiness and peace of mind.

A woman from South America who had been a pilot for many years told me about a powerful dream she had about Amma. She had flown 747s and was usually the co-pilot. She used to think that she was in control of her life – until she had a dream. In the dream, she was sitting at the instrument panel in the plane and turned towards the main pilot. With a jolt, she realized that it was Amma sitting there at the controls. Amma smiled at her and said, "*I am the one that is flying the plane!*" She woke up happy and relieved to know that her life really was safe in the best hands possible.

When we reached Lucknow on the 2006 North India tour, Amma agreed to visit a devotee's house after the evening program had ended. The owner of the house had won a lot of awards for working with disabled people. He had also written numerous books on the subject. One of his sons had been in a wheelchair for many years, since he was 17 years old. Besides being confined to a wheelchair he also had severe breathing problems.

We felt sorrow on seeing the problems of the elder son. Then from the next room the second son emerged. He came very slowly walking towards Amma, step by painful step, assisted by a walker. He suffered from the same debilitating nerve disease that had struck his brother at the same age. It was shocking to see them and how much they both suffered physically.

Amma talked with them, asking them what time they get up in the morning. Both of them told Amma that they wake up at 5:00 a.m., after going to bed at midnight and sleeping five hours. They both held steady jobs. One owned a bookshop and the other worked in a bank. They both always tried to be very cheerful and helpful with the customers. Even though they were extremely disabled, they had the discipline to sleep only five hours and work as hard as anyone else that was healthy and strong. We were all deeply impressed with their surrendered attitude towards life, even though they had the misfortune to suffer so much physically.

At a chai stop earlier on in the tour, a Dutch man had told the whole group traveling with Amma about his experience at the program held just the night before. He had been one of the people helping to control the crowds during the darshan programs. At the end of the evening bhajan, he quickly made his way up to the front of the darshan lines to try and keep the masses inside the fences. The darshan often looked like a city bus in rush hour, crowded with a lot of pushing and pulling. It usually took at least an hour for this initial wildness to settle down.

All of a sudden, a tough-looking man stood in front of him. "Can I go for darshan, quick?" he asked.

"Do you have a token?" he asked him.

"No," said the man, "I am from the police."

He was not wearing a uniform, and the Dutch man had already heard hundreds of reasons why people need to claim a place in the front of the darshan queue: sick mothers, heart conditions, open wounds, disabled children, or just a sad, begging look on their faces.

"Do you have any identification?" the Dutch man asked.

"No, but I have a gun," said the man, as he pointed to his hip.

A little intimidated, the Dutch man moved his hand to the man's hip to check on this. There was indeed a large size pistol there. He started to feel very nervous at this point so he said with a firm tone, "No, you cannot go for darshan with a gun," and slowly pushed the man backwards, wanting to keep him away from Amma and the crowd in case he did something crazy. He was hoping that the man would remain calm. He looked around for someone who could help him out in this delicate situation.

"Can I give you the gun, and then I can go for darshan?" the man asked quite sweetly.

"Yes, you can give the gun to me," the Dutch man replied, figuring at least that way nothing would happen. Five seconds later, he was clumsily holding a large pistol in his hand. He said that he had never held a gun before and was not quite sure how to do it. Finally he was able to see one of the swamis in charge and called him over to help with the situation. This started another long discussion with the man, who eventually was allowed to go for darshan.

In the meantime, other people from the group noticed what was going on and came over to look at the gun that he was holding under his shirt, just like James Bond. A few started to joke, especially wondering why a policeman would want to give his gun to a foreigner.

The policeman returned from his darshan with tears in his eyes. He told how he had driven more than 150 kilometers on his motorbike to meet Amma. If he could not go for darshan with a gun, then he had to go without it. He realized the risk he had taken: if his superiors found out that he had given away his gun, he would lose his job.

At this time, a local politician turned up who was quite famous throughout the state and was also a dedicated devotee of Amma. The policeman had actually been assigned the job of protecting him. He started to lecture the policeman seriously. The policeman looked surprised, then started to smile and finally laughed. He said, "I surrender to Ma, so nothing can happen!" Nobody could argue with that.

Amma says that often people want to follow their own consciousness instead of the Master's words. But our consciousness is rooted in thoughts and the mind and these are rooted in maya and ignorance; so where will we get with all of that? Amma says, "Trust, simply trust in the Guru's existence. Trust in a Perfect Master alone will help you to drop the ego and all egocentric thoughts, enabling you to live life beautifully and embrace death lovingly."

The beauty that permeates our life manifests in the beauty of our death. But this beauty in life is possible only when we surrender to a real Master. Surrendering to a real Master is surrendering to the whole of existence.

Chapter 16

Progressing Spiritually

With all thy getting – get understanding.
Proverbs 4:7

Some people are afraid that if they start to lead a spiritual life more deeply, it will be the end of their freedom. But in truth, when we begin to surrender, it is not the end – it becomes a very beautiful beginning.

When one of the devotees heard that an ashram was being built in California, he had a strong desire to go and live there but also wondered whether he was spiritually strong enough to live in an ashram. He wrote a letter to Amma saying: "I want to see God but I also long to get married and have a family. Should I move to Amma's new center?"

Amma wrote back:

> Amma feels Her son's confusion. Our whole life is a battle against our tendencies. If you want to find out if you are strong enough for ashram life, come and try it. Of course it is possible to live a spiritual life if one is married, but there are more obstacles in the way. If one has the firm conviction that everything only belongs to God and there is

nothing else in the world, then a person can be on whatever path they choose. Whatever path you choose, never doubt Amma is walking with you, holding your hand, guiding you every step of the way.

He was profoundly moved by this letter from Amma, and decided to relocate to California and helped to build the ashram there. Over the years, he has found it to be true that Amma is always holding his hand and leading him in the right direction.

Years ago, one of the devotees was sitting with Amma on a pile of sand in the ashram grounds at Amritapuri. Someone was translating for her. Out of the blue, she playfully asked, "Amma, please tell me my worst fault."

Amma smiled a little but was hesitant to answer. The devotee insisted that Amma tell something. Finally, Amma ventured quietly to answer, "Critical."

The devotee actually burst out laughing and Amma also started to laugh. Afterward, several others who had been watching from a distance questioned her about what had been going on at the time. Seeing Amma and the devotee having such a good time together they had felt a little jealous. Reflecting on this later, she really knew that what made her laugh was – Amma had been exactly right.

She continued telling the story: "Amma nailed me and it was thrilling, absolutely thrilling. The whole time She kept putting my hand on Her shoulder to rub it. I remember Her shoulders felt just like a football player's might have. I would rub Her a little and then I would sneak my hand back, as it was a little awkward for me to be that casual with Amma. But She just kept on pulling my hand back and placing it on Her shoulder again. (I think it was to soften the blow that was coming.) Then She did the most tender thing to me, just like a mother. She gently swept the hair up off of my forehead, like the mom I never had. It was incredibly sweet."

"And then I said 'What else?' thinking that I could handle it and urging Her on. She was very hesitant not wanting to hurt my feelings, but I again insisted, 'What else?' I was extremely puffed up because 'critical' I could handle, so I wanted Her to go on."

"She looked at me, wincingly, as She knew that I was not going to be happy with what followed, but I kept insisting. Finally She said, 'Jealous.' "

"I was not ready for this. I did not see myself that way. I really didn't. So this time I did not laugh. And then She said sweetly, 'Mother is just kidding!' She could see that it was too much for me. Secretly I thought that She was wrong, but years later I realized that She was exactly right."

"After the jealousy part I felt pretty bruised so I said, 'Tell me something good about myself.' I know now that it was a really stupid thing to say. She said, 'No, that would inflate your ego, and flattery is not such a good thing.' "

"Finally, She said something like, 'Don't be like a bug that eats the leaf. Be like a butterfly that gently floats around just bringing joy to people in its short life span.' "

Amma says that all the qualities of God are visible in the actions of a living Guru, and we also can attain these qualities. Through a crystal necklace we can see the thread very clearly. Likewise, God's presence is tangibly manifest in a Mahatma. A Mahatma can act like a mirror that shows us our own true nature in its purest state.

A young woman who had recently been deserted by her husband came to see Amma. She said that there had been no reason at all for him to abandon her. Crying into Amma's lap, she believed that she had not made any mistakes. Amma told her that she must have done something to make her husband unhappy, but the woman was sure there was nothing. In the end, Amma said that a husband wants all of his wife's love and she had not given that. She was shocked, but had to end the conversation there, as her darshan time was over and she had to move to make room for the next person.

Later on, deeply reflecting on what Amma had said, it finally dawned on her what had happened. She remembered that her sister's husband had died a few years before and she had helped to look after her sister's child, bathing, feeding and dressing the baby. Spending so much time with the child, she had grown deeply attached to her. After marriage, she still thought about the child a lot and they spoke on the phone quite often.

Now she understood what Amma had really meant, that she had not given her whole love to her husband. She had forgotten about all of the love, time and attention she had unconsciously given to this child. This revelation came as a jolt to her, but by Amma's grace she became aware of what caused her husband to leave her. Amma deeply understands our shortcomings and the various ways they manifest in our relationships with others. Amma is truly the All-Knowing One.

In the spring following the tsunami, Amma invited several thousands of children to attend two four-day camps at the ashram. One man who lives in the ashram had just been saying that very morning that he could hardly look after his own two children, and he could not imagine having any more than that. But by evening he found himself personally responsible for 100 children. The brahmacharins who came to the ashram to avoid family life were also assigned 100 children each. Some things in life – some prarabdha – we cannot completely escape from, no matter where we may go.

During the camps, all of us were besieged by the number of children running wild in the ashram. They broke potted plants and locked people in their rooms. They made paper airplanes and threw them down over the balconies of the flats, and had pillow fights in their rooms at night, tearing open the pillows and spreading the stuffing everywhere. They were like a second tsunami.

At bhajan time they clapped whenever Amma arrived and left and in between every single song, no matter how many times they were told not to. Their loud clapping reverberated like thunder, drowning out the music. Huge groups of children got up to go to the toilet every few minutes, disturbing the people that were trying to concentrate. They created all different types of havoc. Even though it was hard for most of us to adjust to this chaos, Amma wanted the children who had been through such a difficult time to feel freedom and joyfulness at the ashram. She wanted them to overcome the trauma that they had experienced, and to develop a feeling of closeness with Amma and the ashram, so She was not overly strict with them.

Even though the children seemed to be unmanageable, they were under the protection of Amma. She instructed that the children should have swimming lessons to help them face their fear of the water. One day, one of the women giving swimming lessons to the children felt an overwhelming urge to go to the pool early. When she unlocked the gates of the pool area and entered, she saw a small body floating in the water face-down.

She immediately jumped in the water and pulled the young boy out. A large woman, she usually had trouble getting her own body out of the pool, but luckily she easily and swiftly hauled herself and the boy out of the water onto the side of the pool. She started artificial respiration, and the child was taken off to the hospital.

He recovered extremely quickly. It turned out that this mischievous child had climbed over the wall of the locked area and then jumped into the water, even though he had not been able to swim. Fortunately, this woman had gotten there just in time, and the child was saved.

She later said that there was no reason for her to go early that day, but she felt irresistibly forced to get up from where she was sitting to rush to the pool. She clearly felt that it was Amma's divine intervention that she had arrived at the pool just in time to save the child.

During the four days of the camp, Amma gave the children a chance to speak with Her through question and answer sessions. One child said to Her, "Amma please forgive us, we have been so naughty. Will Amma still bless us even though we have done so many terrible things here?" Amma delightfully replied, "Of course you have Amma's blessings. It is not true that you have been so bad. Amma was much naughtier than you when She was a child." Amma profoundly understood the different layers of consciousness that needed to be addressed in these children. They could have felt abandoned, having lost everything; but instead they gained so much through Amma's forgiving love. At a very deep level, Amma was guiding these children away from the trauma that they had experienced. She was trying to establish a strong foundation of love and

support from the ashram to guide them safely on their journey through life.

As we drove away from Trichy at the end of a South India program in early 2007, Amma noticed some huts built along the side of the road near the highway. She mentioned how sad She feels when She sees people living in thatched huts. It always reminds Her of the difficulties that She saw when She was growing up. She said that whenever She sees individuals living like this, She dreams that everyone in India could have at least a small two-room house to live in, and that they should have at least one good meal to fill their stomach every day.

Although they have a difficult existence, people that live in small villages have the attitude of giving whatever they have to someone who comes to them in need. Usually they have nothing else but food to give, so when guests come to their houses they will always be well-fed. The village people do not think of keeping anything for themselves for tomorrow and usually lead a hand-to-mouth existence. But even though they may have so very little, they still will give away whatever they can to help someone. Amma said that no one ever died of starvation in a village. Somehow the villagers will always look after each other.

Amma explained that village people, even though they may be very poor and have only a few possessions, take great pride in what they have. In the kitchen, their metal cooking pots are cleaned so well that they shine just like a mirror. When Amma was growing up Her mother was very strict with Her while teaching Her how to cook. Not one speck of ash from the cooking fire was allowed to fall into the food, otherwise She would be chastised for carelessness.

Amma's mother always had the customary attitude of receiving guests and offering the best of whatever she could, even if it meant that the rest of the family would go hungry. This generosity came naturally to them. It was not something that needed to be cultivated in villagers of earlier days.

Even now, when poor people come to Amma for darshan, no matter how destitute some of them may be, they will give Her a shawl or a dhoti, as it is their desire to open their hearts by giving something. Some people, if they attain two sets of clothes, will still want to give one set to Her, no matter how little they may have.

As Amma was raised in the village, She has the outlook of a villager, always wanting to give, not thinking about saving anything for tomorrow. This is why when the tsunami struck, Amma wanted to give everything She had. She did not choose to hold anything back for the future. She pledged 23 million dollars, even more than what She had, as She felt confident that She could inspire Her children to work hard to raise what would be needed to fill the deficit.

In 2007, Amma was invited to attend a meeting of the Chief Minister of Maharashtra and top government officials to give advice on how to help reduce the rising incidence of suicide in the country. The government realized that spiritual counseling for the people was needed, alongside with what they could offer, so they turned to Amma for guidance. They were not asking for financial assistance from Amma, but Her compassion for those that are suffering became such that She spontaneously offered aid worth just over 45 million dollars. She is arranging for counseling of people across India, and upliftment of those in the affected areas. When the need presents itself, She can not hold back from trying to help.

Amma feels so desperately sad when She sees the innocent attitude of village people being lost today. The village people's attitude greatly differs from that of the wealthy. The villagers contribute everything when the need is there, unlike the rich, who often feel that they never have enough and always want to accumulate more, right to the end of their lives. No matter how incredibly wealthy people may become, they still have an indelible hunger, yearning for more and more and more. Even to the grave they will never feel content, always thinking about tomorrow and how much they can still acquire for themselves.

The flames from a fire can easily be extinguished, but the flame of endless desire can never be quenched. To crave unendingly for what will never make us happy is such a tragic loss of our precious life energy.

In Japan, a lady confided to me that she was no longer finding any satisfaction in life and that her life seemed filled with endless stress. When I advised that she should try to find a goal in life, she was very surprised, having never thought about this. If we do not have a goal in life we may end up leading an empty life. Going around and around in the cycle of *samsara*, our mind swings like a pendulum from sorrow to joy. Amma assures us that if it swings in one direction then the other is guaranteed to follow.

Amma insists that to find peace we must learn to have the mind under our control, and to do that we need grace. To get this grace we need to perform good actions.

Everyone searches through life to find a little joy and peace of mind to hold on to. We just rarely look in exactly the right place for it. Or when we find the right place, sometimes we don't have the right attitude.

Many years ago when my father was still alive, he decided that he wanted to visit me at the ashram in India. He was in his '70s and apparently wanted more from life. I felt that perhaps he was feeling that he was missing something as he was coming closer to the end of his life. He knew that I had found something very extraordinary in my life and he wanted to experience that for himself. So he decided to do all the same things that I had done in my life that brought me to Amma.

I had traveled through Asia on my own some years before I had come to live with Amma. He decided that he would do this also. He traveled to all the exact same places that I did, on his own as well. But somehow at his older age he did not have similar life-changing experiences.

When he reached India, he came to the ashram to meet Amma. He held out his hand to shake Amma's hand – probably the first person in the world to shake Her hand. I must admit I was very embarrassed at the time but looking back on it now I can appreciate his innocence, as he knew nothing about bowing down or greeting a Saint.

After the handshake, Amma very quickly grabbed him and embraced him in Her own affectionate style of greeting. (I think it was his turn to feel a little self-conscious then.) Next, he shook Amma's mother's hand as well, making her giggle like a little girl. It was quite a funny scene, my father there with Amma in India in his Australian farmer's hat that he always wore.

My father stayed in the ashram for two weeks but could never really understand the profound meaning in life that I had found in Amma's presence. He said that he was too old to change himself. But seeing that I was content and that I had found something that gave real purpose and significance to my life, gave him great happiness. I learned from his experience that we may perform all the same actions as another, step-by-step – but until the heart opens and the ego melts away, we will never find complete peace of mind.

In the fall of 2006, we stopped overnight at Amma's German ashram on the way back from the U.S. Amma called for the group standing outside in the cold trying to catch a glimpse of Her, to come inside and sit. There was snow outside and I was by the door, letting everyone in, until it came to the last one, a dog. I said to it, "Sorry, not you!" But Amma insisted that the dog also come inside. I worried about its muddy feet on the carpet, but Amma did not care.

Amma asked what his name was. It was 'Lucky.' She called out his name a few times and inquired all about him, as She could see that he was not well. She said that dogs only know how to give unconditional love, no matter what we may do to them. We may talk and joke but they will always sit alert and do their job to guard us. They have actually absorbed the essence of spirituality, unconditional love, even more than human beings have.

People wonder how they will know that they are making progress spiritually. Amma says that when we become more expansive, when we develop more patience and compassion and have less anger towards others – this is evidence of spiritual growth. Likewise, if we can maintain an equal state of mind no matter what the external situation brings, we know we are advancing on the path. These are the qualities that we need to attain, so we should focus on cultivating them instead of on other experiences that may come during our sadhana.

Spiritual life is meant to purify us, especially our minds. We think that pollution exists only in the outside world, but the greatest amount of pollution actually lies within us.

The outside world is merely a reflection of our inner world. The negativity that we express through our thoughts, our words and our actions is more powerful than any kind of environmental pollution. They are in fact the most fatal poison. In order to face the challenges of modern life, we must rediscover the inner purifying strength of spirituality.

Chapter 17

The Light in Darkness

*In this dark world, someone has lit a candle. Instead
of complaining about the darkness, follow the light.*
                                        T. Ramakrishnan

A mma says that when sorrows come in life we should try
to turn within and penetrate the surface of our experiences to discover the cause. Sorrow reveals the true nature of
the world. We should try to understand that nobody can love
us more than they love themselves. Nobody will support us
forever. Understanding that God is our only refuge will help
us to become detached in life. We can love others, but if we
become too attached it will always cause us pain.

God has given us the freedom to laugh or cry. Even if we
are completely surrounded by darkness, we should strive to
keep the light within burning brightly. People tend to deal with
tragedies in very different ways. Some may use tragic incidents
to help them change how they live. They are almost forced to
give up their bad habits and lead a more righteous and service-
oriented life. Others may go on replaying a difficult event as
an excuse to escape from life, blaming it for all their failures.

In reality, every problem is like a small seed that has the capacity to sprout and grow into something beautiful. We should learn to use adverse situations in life to grow.

When Thomas Edison was 67 years old, he lost all of his life's work in a fire at his factory, which was not insured for very much. He watched his lifetime's work go up in smoke. Still he tried to look on the bright side of things, realizing that all of his mistakes were also completely destroyed. He said, "Thank God, now we can start anew." Three weeks after this disaster, he still had enough enthusiasm and inspiration to take up his work again. It was at this time that he invented the phonograph.

In 2002, the tribal elders of a small village in Pakistan ordered the gang-rape of a young Muslim woman. The rape was meant to restore her family's honor after her younger brother was accused of being with a girl from a rival tribe. In her country most of the crimes against women go unpunished. She broke her silence and not only pressed charges, but also fought her case right up to the highest court in the nation. When her attackers were found guilty, it sent alarm waves throughout the country. She used the monetary compensation that she was given by the government to build schools in her village.

Now women throughout the country view her as a symbol for hope in the field of women's rights. This shy, uneducated woman could have let the cruel twist of fate destroy her. Instead, she used her misfortune to try to break through the harshness of her culture's ways to help other women. It took inconceivable strength and courage for her to speak out. She was presented with a 'Woman of the Year Award' by Glamour magazine, something she had never even heard of. She used the award prize of $20,000 to help the Pakistan earthquake victims and other women that have gone through similar experiences. She faced her fear and turned it into something that could be the salvation of many others.

When Amma was once asked why She says that sorrow is the greatest teacher, She answered,

> I always considered sorrow as the light in darkness. Millions of people in the world are depressed because they are unable to handle sorrow. But when one pours out that sorrow or sadness to a higher reality or God, it transforms into the pure energy of love. Some amount of suffering will be there in every life, but the real purpose of spirituality is to learn how to handle suffering with grace, ease and a positive attitude. To have the mind under our control we need grace. And to receive grace we need to perform good actions.

We are here on this earth to learn and to progress spiritually. Every situation in life can teach us something important. Each experience that comes to us is the result of our karma. When little difficulties come up in life, somehow we have to persevere and try to work through them. If we can even just *try* to develop the attitude of surrender, then somehow we will gain the grace to overcome any obstacle.

At a program in Kerala, many devotees were sad because a brahmachari refused to give any more darshan tokens for people to see Amma. It was already after midnight and he felt that Amma should take some rest after giving long hours of darshan. He felt that She should not go on and on endlessly seeing people, especially when they had arrived so late in the evening.

Amma felt the opposite. She knew how sad the people would be if they did not receive Her darshan. She also knew that this brahmachari would have to bear the burden of some bad karma for making the devotees experience desperation and sadness at having not received Amma's darshan. To alleviate this karma, She asked him to collect and clean 100 pairs of the devotees' shoes. He managed to obtain about 15 pairs of shoes and wholeheartedly cleaned them. The next morning he gathered and cleaned an additional 100 pairs of shoes. Some people thought it was shameful to see someone in his position cleaning people's shoes, so they went to Amma to express their opinions. Feeling some compassion for him, Amma eventually gave him permission to stop. However, She made quite clear the point that for every action there is a reaction, so we must be extremely careful to consider people's feelings. If our actions intentionally hurt others, then we will have to face some consequences in the future.

Throughout the world innumerable people are suffering intensely. Some have cancer; others lose their families; millions suffer from mental problems. We should be thankful that in comparison with others we experience relatively little suffering. With this thought in mind, we should be grateful for all we have and try to help others in whatever way we can.

In Her early years, Amma witnessed so much intense suffering all around Her; She deeply felt the agony of other people's misery. These experiences made Her understand the ephemeral nature of the world. Seeing the world in this light, Amma wanted to turn away from it. At times, She was so angry at the cruelness of fate that She bit Her body, even drawing blood. Feeling tormented by such senseless suffering, She would pull out Her hair. As an act of martyrdom, She even wanted

to throw Herself into fire and burn away Her own existence, to somehow stop the pain in life.

She would cry out to nature, "I do not want to see all these things!" Sometimes She spoke in a language unknown to ordinary people. Amma said that coarse words would come in Her mouth, but they were not distinct. It was unintelligible, and unlike the earthly language spoken by mortals. Spontaneously it rose up from within Her, and in this way She fiercely admonished nature. With all of these intense feelings of anguish for the suffering of others, She turned away from the world and turned deep inside Her own heart. Her very soul ached to find peace.

Amma always prayed that She should not have even a second of selfishness in Her life, that God should punish Her if She ever did. She cried out to God to give Her the vision to see all as Her Self. She says that this is why today She is never able to feel the difference between men and women. In that sacred vision, She sees all as One. We may not be able to reach the state of seeing all as One, but through cultivating compassion for others, we can start to see ourselves in them.

Only a person who has gone through painful experiences will understand others' sorrows. When we have awareness, every experience, bad or good, contains a lesson for us.

One day, a woman who was always extremely helpful to everyone was called to help a sick neighbor. While she was away, one of her children died in an accident at home. Even though the death was tragic, the woman somehow managed to accept this cruel act of fate.

Two months later, she took her two little boys and her friend's children for a trip to the beach. While she was preparing lunch for everyone, she turned away from the children for a short while and one of her young boys wandered off. She looked for him everywhere, but could not find him. A search party tried to find the boy, but to no avail, and only the next day his young body was found.

The young mother was absolutely devastated after losing two of her children. She could not understand how God could punish her like this. She cried her heart out to a priest at her church, asking why she was being punished like this. Her priest assured her that it was not a punishment from God, but that everything happens for a specific purpose that we may never really understand but have to try to accept.

"But what purpose could there be in this?" she asked tearfully.

The priest thought for a moment and then said, "To whom do all the people in our church go when they are faced with grief or trouble?"

She thought about this for a while, and then said, "They come to me."

"Exactly," said the priest with a smile. "So you see that it is not that God wants to punish you, but when you have experienced so much sadness yourself and survived, you will be able to comfort others who have to go through similar tragedies and sorrow in their lives." This answer helped her find peace.

A family came to Amma with their child who was suffering from leprosy. His little fingers were being eaten away by the disease. They sadly asked Amma if they could consider a mercy killing for the child, as they felt there was no hope for him to survive or even live a decent life.

Amma told them that they should never consider this. If they tried to escape the situation now, they would have to be born again to face the same problem. It was their destiny to learn to feel compassion for the child and to face this pain and suffering, just as it was also the child's destiny to suffer.

Difficulties are not given to us to destroy us – but simply to forcibly bring out the potential that lies within us. If we learn patience, then happiness and peace will eventually follow. Suffering can really help to purify the mind of a devotee.

We should not try to escape situations, but learn to face them with the right attitude.

I have an old childhood friend in Australia who I keep in touch with and receive a letter from every few years. In 2005, she sent me a letter to tell what she was facing in her life. She had been diagnosed with invasive breast cancer and had been rushed to the hospital for an operation to remove her breast, and was going through a several months' course of chemotherapy. Some people faced with this situation would have had many good reasons to be depressed and complain. Instead, she wrote to me the following:

Well, as I am on chemotherapy and all my hair has fallen out, I get to wear a wig. The truth is that my wig is 300% more attractive than my real hair, so I am as keen as mustard to pull the wig on. I look ten years younger – not normal for someone on chemotherapy! Also, if you have to wear a wig, you don't have to wash and blow-dry your hair, so that saves 30 minutes every day on grooming. Being bald makes you swim faster. You save hundreds of dollars on hair coloring, haircuts and shampoo… so there are plenty of good things about being bald. Though, last weekend I learned that one should not go mountain bike riding in a wig. When you rush through the bush, your wig gets taken off by overhanging branches, and then you end up dashing through the bush all bald! And then the dog sees the wig (and well, dogs just adore playing with wigs), so then you spend the rest of the day chasing the dog that's got your hair!

I was so proud of her that in spite of such suffering, she still chose to see the best of the situation and with a surrendered attitude turned her sorrows into laughter.

Sorrows help us to turn inside. When somebody whom we have loved turns against us, we should slowly redirect our attention inward and understand that this is the nature of the world. At these times, we more easily remember that God alone is our refuge.

When we have painful experiences in life, we may tend to react towards others, becoming hurt and angry. Instead, we should direct our pain towards God. In the same way that an oyster uses a painful irritant to make a precious pearl, we also can create something valuable out of a painful experience.

When an Indian devotee's husband died unexpectedly, she decided to go to America and spend some time with her daughter who was living there. Shortly after she arrived in America, she discovered that she needed to have cataract surgery. She was very upset about having this operation in a foreign country, but Amma called her right before the surgery and told Her not to worry, that She would be with her throughout the procedure. During the operation, she had a vision of Amma in Devi Bhava, wearing a beautiful green sari. She was deeply reassured to know that Amma really was with her.

After the surgery, her daughter and son-in-law took her back to their apartment. They settled her in and then left for their jobs, unhappy to leave her alone but without much choice. Soon after they had left, she smelled fragrant roses and jasmine and thought of Amma. She turned and was stunned to see Amma standing in the apartment. Amma wore Her white sari and a jasmine *mala* adorned Her neck. She spent the whole afternoon with her. They walked around the apartment together, talking about the operation and various other things.

Eventually the time came for her daughter and son-in-law to return home from work. She begged Amma to stay a bit longer, as she knew how happy they would be to see Her, but Amma said She had to go. She then asked if Amma would consider leaving behind the jasmine mala as evidence that She had been there, but again Amma said, "No, I have to go now." And then She disappeared.

This woman was thrilled that Amma had come to spend this time with her. Even though she underwent surgery for her eyes, her clear visions of Amma saw her through the challenges of the procedure and the recovery time afterwards.

Amma is the real light in our darkness, illuminating our paths with truth and love and helping us through the hardest times in life. On our part, we must remember to pour out our sorrows to Her alone, knowing that She is our sole refuge.

Chapter 18

Mother of All

There is a primeval Power in this universe. I look upon that Power as my Mother. And even if I choose to be born again a hundred times, She will continue to be my Mother, and I will be her child.

Amma

A poll taken in over 100 non-English-speaking countries asked people to name their favorite word in the English language. 40,000 people returned the poll, and the most popular word chosen was "mother," the sweetest word of all.

A woman does not become a mother just by giving birth. Even a man can become a mother by embodying the nurturing qualities of a mother. Only if one raises children by inculcating proper values and culture in them, does one become a true mother. Traditionally a mother is one who looks after the children: providing them with sustenance, leading them on the path of life and giving them peace and solace.

Amma says that Her motherhood awakened spontaneously in response to the people who came to Her. Like innocent children they looked to Her to solve their problems. They called Her "Mother" so She saw them all as Her children. Seeing Herself as the Mother of everyone, She began embracing people and listening to their problems. Just as sweetness is the inherent nature of any fruit, motherliness, the flow of compassion, is Amma's inherent nature.

Journalists often ask Amma what She feels when She embraces the people who come to Her. Amma replies, "It is not a mere embrace, but one that awakens spiritual principles. It is a very pure experience. I see in people a reflection of Myself. When I look at the people, I become them and feel their sorrows and joys. We meet at the level of love."

So many in today's world want to hurt others and try to gain things only for themselves, but Amma is inspiring millions all around the world to help, love and serve humanity. Even after attaining everything as Amma has, She does not remain inactive, basking in supreme bliss. Amma spends every minute of Her life in the service of others. Every action of a God-realized Soul becomes a blessing to the world, no matter what it may be.

Just as bees are attracted to a sweet-smelling flower, Amma always attracts people to Her wherever She is. Sometimes when we want to stop all the people who run after Her or push into the elevators with Her, Amma may reprimand us. She exclaims, "It is so precious to be able to give someone even just one second of happiness in this lifetime. Shouldn't we do that if we have the chance?"

A famous Indian movie star visited Amma one night while we were in Mumbai. When he entered the room, he went directly over to Amma and started to massage Her shoulders, arms and knees, each for a few seconds. I felt quite offended at this casual display with Amma. But Amma usually sees things differently from us. When I later made an observation about his casualness, Amma disagreed. She said he was someone who really knew how to massage and he could see how tired Amma was. Seeing Her as his mother and out of his innocent love for Her, he spontaneously rubbed Her shoulders to try to make Her body feel better. A mother's heart always sees the best in Her children.

One devotee first came to meet Amma in 1986. He had heard about Amma in his hometown of Mumbai, and when he was visiting Kerala he decided to take a bus to see Her. He was traveling with his son. On the bus, a man sitting next to him asked where he was going. When this man heard they were going to see Amma, he started to talk against Her, saying that She was a CIA agent and giving all sorts of other misinformation.

The new devotee began to get a little scared and thought that maybe someone was trying to make a fool out of him by sending him to meet Her. The man continued talking to him. He said, "A friend of mine met Amma and from the moment he met Her, he left everything, and now he is going to see Her all the time!" When he heard this, he realized that something was probably wrong with this man on the bus, and not with Amma.

When he and his son arrived at the ashram, they found that Amma was giving darshan in the kalari. They had a wonderful darshan and stayed the night. The next morning She called him and gave him a single *rudraksha* bead, and also one for his son. As they were preparing to leave, his son said quietly to him, "Amma should have given two more for my other brothers." His father told him that it was not proper for them to go back and ask for two more. Suddenly Amma called them back and asked the young boy, "How many brothers do you have?"

He replied, "Two." He noticed that Amma already had two rudrakshas in Her hand that She then gave to him.

As they started leaving once more, Amma again called them back. This time She took out a round locket with a chain and told him that when he got home he should give the rudrakshas to his brothers, but he should hold onto the locket until his mother asked, "Did Amma give anything for me?"

When they arrived home, he forgot all about this incident until his mother at last asked if there was anything for her. Then he suddenly remembered and gave her the locket. Even today, 20 years later, she wears this same locket. The whole family became staunch devotees, and Amma has filled their lives with a great deal of joy over the years. They were glad that they did not heed the man's wrongful advice that might have kept them from reaching the all-encompassing arms of their Mother.

A woman from California shared a story about the time she really began to understand Amma's love for her. A few months before Amma's visit to California her grandmother was dying. She showed a photo of her grandmother to a friend and said, "*She* is my mother." In truth, her grandmother had raised her with much more love than she had received from her birth mother. However, she was being very dramatic in trying to explain just how much her grandmother meant to her. It wasn't like a grandmother was dying, but like her *real* mother was dying.

A few months later, after her grandmother had died, she went up to Amma for darshan. Amma told her quite emphatically, *"I am your mother!"* Amma used the same kind of intonation that the woman had used when talking with her friend about her grandmother. It was as if Amma had been there and heard her talk like this, and just wanted to clarify things. She was absolutely stunned by Amma's revelation. It was overwhelming for her to know the strength of Amma's love for her. When she returned to her seat after her darshan, she found that her grief over her grandmother's death had completely vanished. She had lived with this grief for months, and felt that Amma totally absorbed it, as it has never returned.

The crowds at Amma's programs are usually very large. One woman felt totally overwhelmed by the huge crowd when she first went to see Amma. She just hated being in big crowds. When she finally got up to Amma for Her darshan, she asked if Amma really was her spiritual master. Amma replied that indeed She was. Amma knew that she hated being just one in the big crowd, so She replied to her, "If there are 1,000 cows, a farmer would know if even one was missing." The woman could not quite understand this example as she was a city girl from New York and did not have much experience with cows. Amma again explained that She has 1,000 eyes and two of them were only for her. She was happy and relieved to hear this explanation.

Amma has millions of devotees all around the world. Because there are so many of them, some worry if Amma will still be able to take the time to show them personal attention. They wonder if their thoughts and prayers can reach Amma when they are physically far away from Her.

On one occasion someone asked, "Amma, I am afraid that there are so many people calling you that your line will be engaged when *I'm* trying to call you." But Amma assured this person that She has an open connection to everyone all the time; Her line is never engaged. A mobile phone may have limited range, but God's range is unlimited. It does not matter where one may be, because with Amma it is a direct

connection of the heart. Her language is love; She is beyond time and distance and all the other obstacles that we fear may keep us from Her.

At the end of Her satsang at a very large program in South India in 2007, Amma told the devotees that She knows that people complain that they cannot tell Her everything they want to. She sees so many people during the darshan time that often they are limited to only a second or two with Her. She continued, "Amma is not like a doctor or a lawyer to whom you must tell everything. Before God, children do not have to say anything. Amma has the sankalpa that She can hear each and every one of Her children's hearts."

A woman from Seattle related that when her son was six years old, he told Amma that he wanted to be the prime minister of his country. Years later, when he was 20 years old, Amma reminded him of this, and they laughed together about the fond memory.

Amma remembers all Her children no matter where they may be; we should never doubt this.

In America one year, an old Indian man with a long white beard came for darshan. A devotee noticed him and watched his darshan, and later found that he was sitting next to this same man during the evening program. The devotee said hello to him and asked him if he was from India. He answered that he was, and that this was his first trip to America. He had come to visit his son who had moved to America. He said that he had met Amma 14 years before at an Indian program, and had not seen Her since. He then told the devotee that during his darshan, Amma whispered in his ear, "My son, my son, where have you been for 14 years?"

During the U.S. tour, retreats are held in five or six different cities. On the second night of the retreat Amma serves each person a plate of food, then sits with all the young children for a while. The children form a line around Amma's table, and when they walk past Her She feeds each one of them a piece of *pappadam*. Excited and eager parents carry their younger children up to Amma to receive this blessed food from Her.

At the New Mexico retreat in 2006, Amma had finished feeding all the children at the table and was ready to leave the room. One woman, who had three children, had purposely kept her six-month-old baby from getting the pappadam from Amma because Amma was scheduled to give her the first feeding of solid food on the next evening, during the Devi Bhava. As part of this traditional ceremony, Amma takes the baby onto Her lap, and then feeds the baby *payasam* from Her fingers.

When Amma was leaving the room, She saw this woman holding the baby and went straight over to her. Amma was holding a piece of pappadam and asked if the baby had been fed. There was no escaping it – Amma was determined to feed the baby then and there, so She offered her the pappadam. The ever-attentive Mother, She did not want any of Her children to miss out. This baby was so sweet that she ended up getting fed twice by Amma.

At the end of a program in North Kerala in 2006, Amma had seen almost 80,000 people. When the long darshan had finished, Amma still did not have the chance to rest. Devotees had requested Her to visit their homes directly from the program. Amma agreed and visited several places. When all Her engagements had finally finished, Amma proceeded to the vehicle. We were relieved that at last She could take some rest. But surprisingly, Amma requested that She wanted to go to a house where two children had been calling Her to come for a long time. They had lost their mother, so Amma felt sorry for them. It was difficult for us to think of another house visit after all that She had already been through. Even though we insisted that this was not a good idea and pleaded with Her to take some rest, Amma ignored our objections.

Exasperated by Her reluctance to rest, someone made inquiries about the children's house but no one knew exactly to whom Amma was referring. Amma insisted we try to find them – She really wanted to go there. She said that the children always held Her hand on the way to Her room, and had asked Her many times to visit them. She really wanted to fulfill their desire, so She insisted that we try to contact them. Unfortunately, we were unable to find them, so Amma reluctantly gave us permission to continue on our journey.

At the beginning of a foreign tour, while traveling through Sri Lanka in transit, we were in a car on the way to our accommodation. The driver of the car had the radio turned on with some kind of modern music playing. Amma started gently tapping away to the disco music. I thought this was pretty funny as it was not at all Amma's usual kind of music. Amma noticed that I was trying to suppress my laughter, and asked me what was so funny. I mentioned that I had never thought that She was into disco music. Amma smiled and replied that She will see the *devas* inherent in the *raga* of any type of music. In Amma's consciousness, God exists everywhere

In Munich in 2006, red heart-shaped balloons were used to decorate the stage and the hall. At the end of the last program, someone had gathered all the balloons in a big handful and waited outside the entrance to the hall. When Amma finished the program at 9:00 a.m., She went outside and someone gave

Her this beautiful balloon bouquet. She took hold of it and one-by-one slowly let the balloons go. It seemed that She was blessing each one on its way.

The balloons gently drifted up and away. We all watched in wonder for a long time as they drifted up and out into the world, dancing slowly in the wind. It seemed so symbolic. As we drove away with Amma, I kept on looking back at the balloons drifting in the sky in the distance, wondering where they might end up – not knowing how far they might travel, but

knowing that Amma's love went with every single one of them.

After being awake all night for the program, my brain could not quite decipher the deep symbolic meaning of the balloons. But later after a little sleep, when I recalled the memory of this event, I realized that we are all like those heart-shaped, helium balloons. Amma brings us all together for a short time, embraces us and holds us with Her love and best wishes – then She lets us go off into the world again only wanting the best for us, praying for us to reach our real home safely.

An independent, young Israeli man came to visit the ashram on his journey around the world. He was trying to discover what life was all about. He thought Amma was nice but went on his way. He traveled all around India and visited many places. Finally months later he turned up again at the ashram. He had decided to ask Amma what to do with his life because, after seeing everything else, he knew that only She would know the right answer.

Countless people just stumble through their lives. Feeling overwhelmed with pain and sorrow, they inflict pain upon others because they just do not understand what life is all about. I will always be grateful that Amma has given us an understanding of the true nature of the world, and has shown us the joy to be found in trying to lead a life of service to others. We should always remember this very great blessing and try to make ourselves worthy of it. All of the love and grace that has filled our lives should overflow into others' lives as well.

Amma's utter tirelessness never ceases to amaze me. Without a doubt, this world has never witnessed the qualities of humility and compassion, coupled with an overwhelming love for service to humanity, than in the living example of Amma.

Out of the six billion people on this earth we have the grace to come to Amma – just a handful of people out of the whole of this creation. How blessed we are. Amma is offering Her life to try and teach us something incredibly important. We must not let Her life go in vain. It is our duty to try to imbibe something good from Her.

While we were in Spain on the 2005 European tour, a little seven-year-old girl came up to Amma while we were sitting on the stage getting ready to begin the bhajan program. Amma had Her head turned, discussing something with the swami who played the harmonium. The little girl did not want to interrupt Amma, so after waiting for about 15 seconds, she shyly tossed the letter that she had been holding onto Amma's lap, and then quickly ran off the stage.

Amma picked up the letter and opened it. It was written in Spanish in a childish scrawl. Amma wanted to know what it said, so a few of us looked at it, but could not understand the words. As Amma was insistent on knowing what it said, I finally called someone over to translate. The letter said, "*Dear Amma, I love you so very much. Thank you for being the very best part of my whole life.*"

Amma smiled and kissed the letter. She placed it down next to Her for the rest of the program. For the next hour, I kept on periodically looking at the letter in awe, thinking that this little girl had really expressed exactly how most of Amma's devotees feel. In her short life she had actually touched upon an unfathomable truth. I felt that most of us would want to write a letter like this to Amma, conveying exactly everything in those few small words.

"*Dear Amma, I love you so very much. Thank you for being the very best part of my whole life.*"

Glossary

ACHAN: "Father" in Malayalam, the language of Kerala.

AIMS: Amrita Institute of Medical Sciences. Amma's multi-specialty hospital in Cochin.

AMRITAPURI: Amma's main ashram headquarters in Kerala, India.

AMRITAVARSHAM50: Four-day event for world peace and harmony held in Cochin in 2003, for Amma's 50th birthday celebration.

ARATI: Waving the burning camphor with ringing of bell at the end of worship, representing the complete offering of the ego to God.

ASHRAM: A residential community where spiritual discipline is practiced; the abode of a saint.

ATMAN: The Supreme Self or Consciousness. Denotes both the Supreme Soul and the individual soul.

AVADHUTA: One who has realized God but acts more like a crazy person.

BEEDI: A cigarette rolled in dried leaves.

BHAJANS: Devotional singing.

BHAVA: Divine mood or attitude.

BRAHMACHARI: A celibate male disciple who practices spiritual disciplines.

BRAHMACHARINI: The female equivalent of a brahmachari.

BRAHMACHARYA: The practice of self-control of thoughts, words and actions.

BRAHMASTANAM: A temple where the central deity is made up of four different sides (Ganesh, Shiva, Devi and a serpent) representing that all are different aspects of the same One. The idea of this unique form of worship was created by Amma.

CHAI: Indian tea boiled with milk.

CHILLUM: A pipe made of clay used to smoke tobacco or intoxicants.

DARSHAN: Vision of the Divine or audience with a holy person.

DEVI: Divine Mother.

DEVI BHAVA: "The Divine Mood." The state in which Amma reveals Her oneness and identity with the Divine Mother.

DHARMA: Duty or righteous responsibility.

DHOTI: Piece of cloth wrapped around the waist usually worn by men.

EGO: Limited "I"-awareness, which identifies with limiting attributes such as the body or the mind.

GURU: A spiritual teacher.

KALARI: The small temple where Amma originally held the Bhava Darshans.

KARMA: Action or deed. Also the chain of effects that our actions produce.

MAHA SAMADHI: When the life force is completely withdrawn from the body.

MAHATMA: Literally "Great Soul." A Hindu title of respect for a spiritually elevated person. In this book, Mahatma refers to a God-realized soul.

MALA: A necklace or garland.

MALAYALAM: Amma's mother tongue. The language of Kerala.

MANTRA: A sacred sound or group of words with the power to transform.

MAUNAM: Keeping a vow of silence.

MAYA: Illusion.

OM NAMAH SHIVAYA: Powerful mantra with different interpretations, usually meaning, "I bow down to the Eternally Auspicious One."

PADA PUJA: Traditional worship ceremony of washing the Guru's feet.

PAPPADAM: Very popular, thin, round, crisp food item usually served with rice.

PEETHAM: A sacred seat.

PRANAM: A form of greeting in India. The palms of the hands are pressed together at the level of the heart, with the fingertips touching the forehead. This is a modification of a full prostration, showing respect.

PRARABDHA KARMA: The fruits of actions from previous lives that one is destined to experience in the present life.

PRASAD: A blessed offering or gift from a holy person or temple.

PULISHERI: A liquid made from boiled yoghurt with turmeric and spices, made to eat with rice.

PUJA: Ceremonial worship.

RAGA: A melodic pattern of notes in Indian music expressing a certain mood.

RUDRAKSHA: Seed of a tree usually grown in Nepal that is known for its medicinal and spiritual power. Legendarily known as "teardrops of Lord Shiva."

SADHANA: Spiritual practices that lead to the goal of Self-realization.

SADHU: A holy person.

SAMADHI: Oneness with God. A transcendental state in which one loses all sense of individual identity.

SAMBAR: A mixture of chili and spices cooked with vegetables.

SAMSKARA: Samskara has two meanings: Culture, and the totality of impressions imprinted in the mind by experiences (from this or earlier lives), which influence the life of a human being – his nature, actions, state of mind, etc.

SANATANA DHARMA: Literally "eternal religion." The original and traditional name for Hinduism.

SANKALPA: A resolve.

SANSKRIT: Ancient Indian language.

SANYASSIN: One who has taken the formal monastic vows of renunciation. They wear ochre colored cloth to represent the burning of all worldly attachments.

SARS: Severe Acute Respiratory Syndrome.

SATSANG: Listening to a spiritual talk or discussion; the company of saints and devotees.

SEVA: Selfless service.

SIDDHA YOGI: Literally "one who is successful." One who has attained the state of Self-realization.

SUGUNACHAN: Amma's biological father (Sugunanandan achan).

SWAMI: One who takes the monastic vows of celibacy and renunciation.

TABLA: A North Indian drum set.

TAPAS: Austerity, hardship undergone for the sake of self-purification.

TULASI: Holy basil, a medicinal plant.

UNNIAPPAM: Deep-fried sweet popular in Kerala.

VASANAS: Residual impressions of objects and actions experienced, latent tendencies.

VEDANTA: Literally "end of the Vedas," a system of philosophy based on the teachings of the *Upanishads*. Vedanta declares that God is the only reality and that creation is essentially an illusion.

VIBHUTI: Sacred ash, usually given by Amma as prasad.